RONALD LEE HANCOCK

A Screenplay, a Teleplay, a Foreign Film, A Stage Play and an Epic Movie

A SCREENPLAY, A TELEPLAY, A FOREIGN FILM, A STAGE PLAY AND AN EPIC MOVIE

iUniverse books may be ordered through booksellers or by contacting:

iUniverse
1663 Liberty Drive
Bloomington, IN 47403
www.iuniverse.com
1-800-Authors (1-800-288-4677)

Because of the dynamic nature of the Internet, any web addresses or links contained in this book may have changed since publication and may no longer be valid. The views expressed in this work are solely those of the author and do not necessarily reflect the views of the publisher, and the publisher hereby disclaims any responsibility for them.

Any people depicted in stock imagery provided by Thinkstock are models,
and such images are being used for illustrative purposes only.
Certain stock imagery © Thinkstock.

ISBN: 978-1-4917-6479-4 (sc)
ISBN: 978-1-4917-6480-0 (e)

Library of Congress Control Number: 2015905287

Print information available on the last page.

iUniverse rev. date: 06/08/2015

To my wife, my daughter, and my grandson

CONTENTS

PREFACE

The following plays are derived from various writings by the author. Firstly, "Wave of Destiny" is a script for a full length movie; "What's in a Name" is an hour teleplay; "The Pepper Grinder" is a stage play that the author has already produced in Reno, NV.; "A Writer's Mind" is a collection of a variety of writings, some already published, some not., none in screenplay format; and lastly "Chinese Blossom Notes" is written as a foreign film that would be inexpensive to produce. These plays are registered and available for production.

I

WAVE OF DESTINY

Registration #1447413

Introduction

This play is a movie script and has had the trailer produced at Lake Tahoe by a Hollywood producer. Nothing else has been developed.

The storyline has a plot within a plot. There are two changes from black and white to color film. The first color change occurs during a make believe plot of a play that the main character is discussing with a colleague . The second time involves the main female character in the overall plot in which she appears to drown and at that instant there is a color change while panning up her arm as she is being carried from the water. The film changes from color after a fireworks scene back to black and white at the clinic scene.

FADE IN:

1. INT/LIVING ROOM—DAY

> VERN (A friend of Kenneth)

It will do you good to get away from Kansas City. You've been moping around long enough after the passing of your wife.

> KENNETH

Yeah, in a way the opening of my play "You and I Make Three" in New York City will give me reason to leave here.

1

VERN

Don't worry about the house. I will try to sell off as much of your stuff as possible and after the realtor sells the place, I'll put the rest in storage.

KENNETH

Descent of you old man. I'll keep in touch with you. You can always catch me on the 'cell'. Well I'll be in New York City by 10:00PM tonight. I'll call you when i'm sure of where I will be staying. Goodbye and again thanks for everything. You've been a good friend.

2. INT/HOTEL LOBBY—NIGHT

KENNETH

I made reservations here but I'm a day early. Kenneth Farnsworth. I hope you have something.

DESK CLERK

No problem Mr. Farnsworth. Room 576. Bell boy front desk.

3. INT/HOTEL ROOM—NIGHT

KENNETH

Vern, I'm safe and sound at the Fifth Avenue Hotel which is close to the theater. Flight went well. I hope the rest of my life goes that smoothly. O.K. I won't keep you any longer. Bye, bye.

4. INT/THEATER—DAY

[Scene] A rehearsal is in progress as Kenneth walks towards the stage. Seated in the third row Is the Director, Jason and in the 5th row is his assistant, Jane.

KENNETH

Hi, Jason. How are things going?

JASON

Kenneth! Didn't expect you here this early. When did you get into town? Oh, by the way this is Jane. This is Kenneth, the playwright.

KENNETH

Glad to meet you. Actually I arrived yesterday. I wanted to make sure I got here in time for the opening night and you've been having quite a bit of nasty weather recently.

JASON

Take ten (to the actors on stage). Come with me Kenneth to the backstage. I want you to meet our leading lady. [A moment later] Shirley this is the playwright Kenneth Farnsworth.

SHIRLEY

Oh, my. I've heard a great deal about you.

KENNETH

Oh, my, I've heard a great deal about <u>you</u>. Actually your name and back-ground came up during a casting meeting. We had seen your C.V. and were very impressed. We're lucky to have you. I recall you're married. Is your husband in New York with you?

SHIRLEY

No, he is working in Indianapolis--our home town.

Opening night is successful and Shirley and Kenneth become close friends.

5. INT/BACK THEATER—DAY

KENNETH (To Shirley)

Do me a favor and instead of that two hour lunch break in the backrooms, walk with me in Central Park and starve. Just kidding. We could bring our lunches with us.

SHIRLEY

Sure, sounds like fun.

6. EXT/CENTRAL PARK—DAY

KENNETH

I find you to be clever. So what I want you to do is to help me with a screenplay that I am writing. Each day at noon, since you have nothing else to do- ha, ha, sorry about this, but you can always say no. I will understand but we can be resting on a bench while getting some fresh air and possibly getting wet. We could run over to a café if that were the case. O.K.?

SHIRLEY

No problem. It will do me good to get outside.

KENNETH

Well to get us started—the play begins with at a cocktail party, of course.

7. INT/APARTMENT—NIGHT

[Scene] Howard sees the most gorgeous woman he has ever laid eyes on. She is Hispanic and in a wheel chair and at the moment is not talking with anyone. Howard approaches.

HOWARD

I…I…ah…

CYNTHIA

Maybe I should start the conversation.

HOWARD

Yes, please help me out here.

CYNTHIA

My name is Cynthia Mason and yours is …?

HOWARD

I'm working on it. Oh my gosh you are a beautiful woman. Sorry to be so impolite and bumbling but you have captured my breath and my mind.

CYNTHIA

I know who you are anyway Howard K. Steel.

HOWARD

That's been the story of my life. I'm always surrounded by smart people. Cynthia laughs.

8. EXT/CENTRAL PARK—DAY

SHIRLEY

They need to get out of the cocktail party and be alone somewhere, say at a restaurant. But how? Oh just push the wheelchair out of there.

KENNETH

Yes. What about their returning to her apartment with the assistance of a lady with her at the cocktail party that she normally has with her. Then they all go to the apartment where the lady cooks a candle-light dinner for them.

SHIRLEY

Have them travel even though she is paraplegic.

KENNETH

Good idea. But first I'm going to have him move in and have them live together for some time on the ploy that he says she needs protection in the mean, bad city. In this way he has time to begin falling in love with her.

9. INT/APARTMENT—DAY

HOWARD

I'm taking you away from New York and we're going fishing and boating, but we're going to travel by train.

CYNTHIA

What?

10. INT/TRAIN COMPARTMENT—DAY

HOWARD

Now isn't this a lovely way to travel? We'll have dinner soon. I'll carry you afterwards to the club car and we'll drink ourselves a little silly.

11. EXT/ CENTRAL PARK—DAY

KENNETH

This is our third session out here and I keep forgetting to comment about your hair color Shirley. Its auburn isn't it?

SHIRLEY

Yes, so what is so fascinating about that?

KENNETH

I don't know but that ah…I can't think of what to say about it, but it's the reddish tinge in it that is ah, ah

SHIRLEY

Bothersome?

KENNETH

Precisely. That's it. It bothers me. But how and why? I'm cracking up, I guess. It's a mystery to me. Something in my past.

SHIRLEY

Something in your future? Well it about time you gave a girl some notice, even if you don't have any idea of what you are saying.

KENNETH

Sorry. Besides you're a married woman. Let's get back to business. Oh, we can't. It's time for you to get back to the theater.

12. INT/TRAIN CLUB CAR—NIGHT

Howard carries Cynthia from the dinner car after a sumptuous British Columbian salmon dinner to the club car and places her gently down in one of two lounge seats arranged in a circle where there are several others already seated.

HOWARD

Let me introduce Cynthia and my name is Howard.

STAN

Stan.

GLORIA

Gloria-Stan's best half. The other two you don't need to know their names. They're 'no goods'

JACK

I'm Jack, the no good, and this is my girl Elisabeth.

CYNTHIA

We're glad to meet you all.

Cynthia and Stan order two brandies on the rocks.

STAN

So where're you two off to?

HOWARD

To San Fran. Just for a visit.

STAN

What line of work are you in?

HOWARD

Cynthia has been a film editor and I'm a retired film director.

CYNTHIA

Howard likes to impress people. I'm just a librarian now, deep down in the bottom floor amongst the dusty volumes.

13. EXT/CENTRAL PARK—DAY

SHIRLEY

After the fishing trip, I think they might go somewhere really exotic for a paraplegic—to Mount Hood. Let them fly, say, by helicopter.

KENNETH

Excellent.

[Scene] Cynthia and Howard get off the train at St. Louis and hire a bush pilot to fly them to the Ozarks to a particular camp that Howard has contacted by phone. He carries her out of the plane after a bumpy ride and even bumpier landing on the lake. Then he proceeds to take her out of the plane after it taxies up to the dock. He next places her on a bench in the office and they buy some fishing gear and food.

14. INT/CAMP OFFICE—DAY

CYNTHIA

Is there cooking ware and bedding in the cabins?

CAMP MANAGER

Yes. I think everything you'll need is there except for "Bug Off". Here I'll throw a couple of spray cans in free of charge.

HOWARD

Thanks. Now which boat is for us and the location of the cabin is just around that rocky point. Right?

CAMP MANAGER

Number seven and yes.

HOWARD (lifting Cynthia from the bench)

I couldn't have said it any more succinctly myself.

[Scene] Their stay is uneventful. Cynthia catches her first fish sitting with a life vest on the small dock outside their cabin and there are boating and cooking scenes.

15. EXT/CENTRAL PARK—DAY

SHIRLEY

O.K. They fly from the lake after say three days; back to St. Louis and by plane to San Fran where they take a tourist helicopter package to Mount Hood.

[Scene] Landing on one side of Mount Hood at about 13,000 feet.

KENNETH

Let's put in a scene of them in the snow.

16. EXT/MT. HOOD—DAY

[Scene] Howard carries Cynthia out into the bright sunlight. The reflection is blinding and the snow is blowing. Howard sets Cynthia down into about four and a half feet of snow.

CYNTHIA

I'm standing upright all by myself for the first time in my life!
Just leave me here—just go on. I never want to leave this position.

HOWARD

(Takes a few photos of Cynthia and then yells against the wind…)

I'm in love with you!

CYNTHIA

I can't hear you.

HOWARD

Yes you can and you did.

CYNTHIA

Oh, HOWARD, you're so wonderful to me.

17. EXT/CENTRAL PARK—DAY

SHIRLEY

Kenneth, is Howard married?

KENNETH

Yes.

SHIRLEY

Well then let's have his wife track down her 'wily' husband Howard, who is supposed to be in New York at the theater. First she finds out he left with Cynthia to go fishing at the camp in the Ozarks. I'm not sure how she finds this particular place.

KENNETH

He has left a forwarding address with the theater manager.

SHIRLEY

The camp manager overheard their plans to go to Mt. hood. But that would simply lead them astray since they are in San Fran.

KENNETH

Yeah, that is puzzling. She would have to go to San Fran and check around the yellow pages on getting trips to Mt. Hood. But instead she realizes she only needs to simply check out the hotels for her Howard Steel. That should do it.

18. INT/ SUITE AT JACKSON HOTEL—DAY

HOWARD

What's wrong Cynthia? I don't understand I love you beyond belief and you love me. Why can't we figure things out? Why can't we be happy together?

CYNTHIA

I know this sounds weird but I don't understand you. You take care of me completely You dress me, you undress me, you take care of my feminine hygiene needs, you bath me, you would fix my hair and put on my makeup if I even would let you. You're too much and I can't even give you sex. You're smothering me with your love. I can't, I can't stand it any longer.

HOWARD

But I love you. Therefore it's no effort for me to do these thing for you.

19. INT/HOTEL BATHROOM—DAY

[Scene] Cynthia begins screaming in the bath tub as Howard gets ready to give her a bath. Cynthia notes feces floating in front of her. She begins smearing feces on the wall in agony. Howard enters the bathroom to ascertain the commotion and sees what she's doing. Howard picks up a piece of floating feces and smears it on the tip of Cynthia's nose.

HOWARD

Now let it be understood. No amount of feces is going to change my love for you. So just forget these antics.

20. INT/HOTEL BEDROOM—DAY

Howard doggedly cleans Cynthia with no words being spoken and places her on the bed, dries her and dresses her. Cynthia stops sobbing.

HOWARD

Now we're going across the street and have a huge portion of crab salad and a large glass of California Chablis and you're going to fall in love with me.

There is a knock on the door. Howard opens it.

Marlene!

Closing the door behind him and stepping out into the hallway.

21. INT/HOTEL HALLWAY—DAY

MARLENE

Yes it is Marlene and your going back with me this very moment- you philanderer.

HOWARD

A little later you may not like those words. Now be civil and come meet Cynthia.

They return back into the hotel suite.

22. INT/HOTEL SUITE—DAY

HOWARD

Sit over on that chair please (to Marlene).

Howard hears Cynthia crying. He enters the bedroom.

23. INT/BEDROOM—DAY

HOWARD

What's the matter darling.

CYNTHIA

Your wife will take you away from me.

HOWARD

Now look directly into my eyes and listen carefully what I am about to say. I am never going to leave you. (With a stern voice)

He wipes her face gently with a tissue.

Now, let's go meet Marlene.

Howard picks her up off of the bed. Cynthia is still sobbing slightly.

Marlene this is Cynthia. Cynthia this is my wife.

MARLENE

Why, she's crippled!

HOWARD

Paraplegic is a kinder word.

MARLENE

And she is a dark-skinned Latino.

HOWARD

So? Incidentally, she is from the Philippines and is therefore Hispanic not from Latin America.

MARLENE

Why you have been crying dear. What is the matter?

HOWARD

She's frightened of you.

MARLENE

Please don't be scarred of me. I simply want my husband back.

HOWARD

We were just going to have lunch. Please join us Marlene. The three of us have a lot to talk about.

24. INT/RESTAURANT—DAY

(After lunch)

HOWARD

Marlene I want you to do me a big favor and take Cynthia shopping. I promised I would take her today. I have no excuse not to be with you two, but this will give both of you an opportunity to know each other. She will tell you what to do. I will be indebted to you for a lifetime if you would do this for me Marlene.

25. INT/HOTEL SUITE—DAY

(When they return)

HOWARD

Now, that wasn't so bad was it? Or was it? How much stuff did you two buy?

MARLENE

And more is being delivered. They have fantastic shops here.

HOWARD

I have to clean Cynthia up a bit and then we can all chat some more. Marlene I want you to be thinking about staying here for a while, a few days that is. We'll discuss this a little later. O.K.?

[Two weeks later]

MARLENE

Howard, I have never met a nicer person in my life and that includes you mister. She is adorable in every way. I understand how you fell in love with her. I bow to your relationship. Only, let me have a favor now from you. Let me stay with you two. I will try not to be in the way. You realize I am in a position to be a bitch.

HOWARD

You're not a bitch, you're an angel. It is precisely what I wanted to happen. Cynthia needs both of us for her mind and body. I'm sure she would be delighted. We'll get us a bigger place somewhere and all of us will call it home.

[Ending scene]

26. EXT/SAN FRAN PARK—DAY

Marline has hold of one of the wheelchair handles and Howard has his hand on the other side, as all three of them are going down a park lane.

27. EXT/NEW YORK CENTRAL PARK—DAY

KENNETH

That does it. Thank you so much Shirley. I've decided to go to my get-away spot in the Virgin Islands. Let me invite you and your husband to my coastal cottage there for any amount of time you and your husband can spare with me. Please say you'll come after the play ends this summer. I promise not to make you work on my screenplay. And besides I would be very lonely not seeing you again.

SHIRLEY

Oh, it's been fun. I'll miss you too Kenneth. And you can read whatever you like into that.

Shirley kisses Kenneth on the lips and says goodbye. Kenneth rents a car the next day and heads south down the Atlantic coast with the intention of flying from Miami to the Virgin Islands, after contacting his old buddy, his past agent—Burney.

FADE OUT

FADE IN

28. INT/ CINDY'S HOUSE-DAY

STEP MOTHER

Cinderella! Get your ass down here immediately and get the kitchen floor cleaned.

CINDY

(Coming down the stairs from her bed room and enters the kitchen)

I told you not to call me Cinderella.

STEP MOTHER

You don't tell me anything young lady. I tell you what I want to tell you. Now get to work.

The step mother leaves the kitchen and two step sisters enter from the outside door into the kitchen.

ALICE

Well, how's it going Cindy. Any dates for tonight?

CINDY

None of your business and look what your doing, tracking in mud over floor area that I have just cleaned. Thanks a lot sisters (sarcastically).

SHARON

Too bad.

The step mother returns.

STEP MOTHER

Get out of the kitchen you two so I can start lunch. Are you about through Cinderella? What did I overhear you say about a date tonight? Not unless you get the house work finished. I have afternoon tea coming up with the ladies tea party tomorrow. It's my turn to have it at my place.

CINDY

But Sid and I were going to...

STEP MOTHER

To what? So his name is Sid is it? I'll put a stop to this nonsense. Keep working.

SALLY AND SHARON

(Who have not left the kitchen, yet)

So Cindy's got a boy friend, a boy friend, a boy friend. (teasingly).

STEP MOTHER

Get out of here I said and go straighten up your rooms.

[Later]

29. EXT/SID'S CAR—NIGHT

CINDY

I've got to get out of here. You've got to help me. Do you love me?

SID

Of course I do.

CINDY

Well then here's my plan. Each day we meet at school and you take me in your pickup. I'll have smuggled out of my room items, say clothing, or something that I need. I'll give you a small suit case and you'll have it tucked away behind the front seat here. It will just be a matter of adding things to it each day until I'll be ready. O.K.?

SID

Sounds good on your part. Does that mean I'll never ever see you again?

CINDY

Oh, we'll meet again, I'm sure, especially if the cops find me. I won't be able to write you because then they'll be able to trace me. Oh, please understand, I've got to get away or there won't be anyone called Cindy or any name- no matter what.

SID

I'm going to miss you. So when do we begin?

CINDY

Tomorrow.

[Two weeks later]

30. EXT/HIGH SCHOOL—DAY

CINDY

That's it. I'm ready. Don't take me home. Take me as far south as you can and drop me off.

[Scene]

The pickup nears a roadside café.

> Go on past here a bit. There may be someone in the café that knows me. I guess this is it. Let me have your bottle of water. Goodbye Sid. I will always think of you. They kiss.

SID

> Goodbye Cindy.

[Scene]

Cindy steps out of the pickup and Sid reaches over with the suitcase. They wave at each other as Sid's turns his pickup around and starts back home.

CINDY (to herself)

> I guess I will hitchhike on south as fast as I can. They'll start searching for me right away.

FADE OUT

FADE IN

31. EXT/FILLING STATION—DAY

While he has stopped at a filling station, near Richmond, Virginia, Kenneth notices a poster on a bulletin board. It is an amateur play 'When Love Was Born', being performed tonight at the University of Richmond. Kenneth is immediately attracted to seeing the play and realized he needed a good break from driving.

KENNETH (to the gas attendant)

How do I get to the University of Richmond from here?

ATTENDANT

Well, it's a little tricky. You need to continue south on Interstate 95 but take the turn off onto interstate 195. Then a right on 147 which is a state highway and is actually in town called Carey Street. You know I don't really know myself. It's probably about two miles to another right onto some road to the university. Better ask someone around there—another filling station perhaps. Sorry.

FADE OUT

FADE IN

[Scene]

Soon a truck stops and the driver asks Cindy where she is heading. Cindy climbs in and soon falls asleep. The truck stops at a truckstop.

32. EXT/ROADSIDE CAFÉ-NIGHT

FIRST TRUCK DRIVER

Wake up little girl. This is as far as I go.

CINDY

Where are we?

FIRST TRUCK DRIVER

Ashland, Virginia.

CINDY

Thanks

She goes in the café and has a Pepsi, then steps outside. A big burley man appears.

FADE OUT

FADE IN

KENNETH

Oh, that'll be fine. I'm sure I will be close enough to find it now.
Thanks.

Kenneth proceeds to the campus where the play will be presented but needs to wait a little over two hours, so he has dinner at the university café. It is quite crowded. Three students offer him a seat with them at their booth. After introductions they learn that all of them are going to the play.

FADE OUT

FADE IN

33. EXT/OUTSIDE TRUCK STOP CAFÉ-NIGHT

SECOND TRUCK DRIVER

Need a lift? Which direction you going?

CINDY

South.

SECOND TRUCK DRIVER

Hop in. I'm going as far as Fayetteville, North Carolina.

CINDY

O.K., great.

[Later]

SECOND TRUCK DRIVER

You don't talk much do you? How old are you anyway?

His right arm swings over onto her belly.

CINDY

Knock it off.

SECOND TRUCK DRIVER

Oh come on. I get lonely out here.

His hand enters the upper part of her panties under the elastic.

CINDY

Well, at least stop driving and pull over off the road, over by those trees.

34. EXT/WOODS-NIGHT

[Scene]

The truck driver stops the truck; Cindy moans and slides downwards in the seat as the driver begins to bring her to an erotic climax; she murmurs a slight scream; he ejaculates into his jeans; then reaches across and opens the door pushing her out onto the dirt and tosses her backpack beside her.

Second Truck Driver

I've had enough of you kid.

And drives this truck away back onto the highway.

CINDY

(to herself after she hears the truck pull away out on the highway)

I will kick some leaves together right here by this rock overhang and tuck myself in for the night.

FADE OUT

FADE IN

35. EXT/CAR-NIGHT

After the play, Kenneth offers to drive them back to their universities. They had come by bus.

DON

Well, what did you think of the play?

KENNETH

I would have been more conservative and I would have ruined it. By the way, the leading lady in the play is a red head?

DON

Yes, that was Jo Ann. Why do you ask? Well the leading lady in my Broadway play is a red head. I wonder what the probability of that is.

SANDY

Probably pretty low.

KENNETH

I know for a fact that only one or two percent of the world population has red hair. I imagine that would hold true for the female population. Say one out of one hundred people that would be cast for that lead part would be redheads and here I am finding two female leads as red heads. Ummm…

JOE

Do you multiply 0.01 by 0.01 to get 0.0001 or therefore 0.01 percent probability between the two plays?

KENNETH

You got me. I'm just a playwright. Incidentally I'm a romantic. I know that plays began with the Greeks who defined two types-- tragedy and comedy. Euripides was the first playwright of Greek tragedy and Aristophanes was the genius of Greek comedy, but I don't know anything about my own area that of romance. The history of the romantic play was obviously before Shakespeare I'm sure--probably in Roman times. So you all know each other but Sandy you and Don are steadies going to the University of North Carolina and Jo you are studying at the University of Richmond. What's your majors?

DON

I don't really know, but I may go into theater management.

SANDY

I 'm studying for a biology major.

JO

I'm in pre-nursing.

KENNETH

Really--a humanitarian in our presence. That's nice. Where would you study for your RN certification?

JO

Maybe up at the University of North Carolina.

KENNETH

By the way you'll need to direct me pretty soon to the University
of North Carolina campus in Chapel Hill.

Sandy and Don say their thanks as they get their things in the back. Soon Kenneth and Jo arrive in Fayetteville University and Jo gets his backpack and thanks Kenneth for the ride and that it was a privilege meeting him.

36. EXT/ STREET—DAY

FADE OUT

FADE IN

37. EXT/WOODS-DAY

The sun flickers upon Cindy's face through the trees and she awakens and walks back out to the highway. Several cars pass but soon a pickup truck with a lady driver stops.

THIRD TRUCK DRIVER

Need some help there?

CINDY

Yes, fine. Where are you going?

THIRD TRUCK DRIVER

I'm heading for Osborn, South Carolina.

CINDY

If I may.

She climbs into the right seat, buckles up.

I appreciate this. I'm meeting a cousin in a town near there. I thought I'd save my money by hitchhiking.

THIRD TRUCK DRIVER

Yeah, but it might cost you your life. That's pretty darn expensive.

CINDY

You're right of course. How far is it to Osborn?

THIRD TRUCK DRIVER

Far enough, but not too far.

[Scene]

Soon they arrive at the outskirts of Osborn and Cindy wave's good-bye, as she walks into town, a young man approaches her.

MAN

Say, little lady. How'd you like to work for me? Looks to me like you could use some quick bucks

Kenneth stops at a roadside restaurant in the small town of Osborn, in South Carolina. As he sits eating his sandwich, he notices across the street a scuffle occurring between a young man and a teenaged girl. Kenneth immediately passes through the glass door and walks briskly across the street yelling.

KENNETH

Will you hurry up? I've been waiting for you for over twenty minutes now?

The surprised girl quickly takes the cue.

JAN/CINDY

I'm coming. I'm coming.

38. INT/ RESTAURANT—DAY

Now that she is across from him in a booth he notices two things. One is that the man has disappeared and secondly, the girl is filthy and has a disheveled appearance,

KENNETH

Why don't you go into the ladies room and clean up a bit and I'll order you something to eat?

She scampers off. The waitress appears.

WAITRESS

That guy across the street-he's a bit of a pimp, trying to do a quick invitation. What you did mister probably saved her life from the streets.

KENNETH

Let me order two hamburgers and fries for her, O.K.?

The girl returns from the restroom looking a little better.

KENNETH (to the girl)

So where are you headed for?

JAN

Oh, nowhere in particular.

(Pause)

KENNETH

I hope you won't take this the wrong way, but my wife passed away about four months ago and I'm just traveling around. To be perfectly candid, I'm lonely and you'll be hungry again soon. If you think you can trust an old goat like me, we'll get a place to stay and you can clean up. Tomorrow I'll buy you some decent clothes and we'll think of what's next. You'd be doing me a great favor. What do you say? Please say yes.

JAN

Sure, sounds great. Shouldn't I be begging you to give me a deal like this? Of course I'll go with you. I need you more than you need me.

KENNETH

Good then let's find a nearby place —or better yet, I think the next town south is a little bigger and we can get a nicer motel. We can also get away from your new friend. I like you already. I sense that we're going to be great friends.

JAN

I've never seen that guy before.

KENNETH

If you want to you can take that other hamburger with you and
we can leave right after you have finished.

[Scene driving to next town]

After spotting a motel and checking in, Jan enjoys a long hot shower, hops into one of the beds and
was out. Kenneth allows her to sleep until about five o'clock and then wakes her.

KENNETH

Let me take you to a clothing store and get you something to wear
this evening when we go to a nice restaurant. Incidentally, you
look almost human now. Have you been on the road a long time?

JAN

Yes, but I don't want to talk about it.

KENNETH

Fine, I don't really care. You can call me Uncle Kenneth and I
don't want to know your real name. I decided to call you Jan.

JAN

I like my new name. Thanks.

KENNETH

Looks like we'll have to get you to the coiffures too.

JAN

What's that?

KENNETH

A hair dresser.

39. EXT/CLOTHING STORE—DAY

They arrive at the clothing store. A saleslady greets them promptly.

KENNETH (to the saleslady)

She needs some general wear and some beach clothes.

JAN

Beach clothes?

KENNETH

Yes, I'll tell you about it later

[They look around at a few clothes-scene]

Kenneth pays with cash.

Is there a beauty parlor near- by?

SALESLADY

Yes. Just two stores down to your left.

Jan has her hair cut.

KENNETH (to himself)

She is rather an attractive girl after that striking shorter style.

40. EXT/ SIDEWALK—DAY

KENNETH

How old are you?

JAN

Sixteen.

KENNETH

A wonderful age to be independent, if you have money to eat on.
I'm 52 and I know where my next meal is coming from. Although
I will have to admit I would like to be sixteen again. I'm really
quite envious of your age Jan.

41. EXT/ SIDEWALK—DAY

Kenneth approaches a man on the sidewalk outside the clothing store.

KENNETH

Pardon me sir. Can you tell me where the nicest restaurant in
town is?

MAN

That would be the Shell Fish restaurant. Two blocks over that way.

KENNETH

Thank you very much.

JAN

I'm starving.

KENNETH

Start getting use to calling me Uncle Kenneth.

JAN

O.K. Uncle Kenneth, but I'm still starving.

42. INT/ MOTEL-DAY

Jan puts on her new dress as Kenneth watches.

KENNETH

A bit of a butterfly metamorphosis, I would say.

They enter the Shell Fish restaurant and sit at a cozy booth.

43. INT/ RESTAURANT—NIGHT

KENNETH

I hope you like shellfish. Let me order for both of us. Hi. (as the waiter approaches). We will start with the mixed sea fish soup for both of us and then next we should like to have grilled mussels. We'll order more after that. Ice tea Jan?

JAN

That will be fine Uncle Kenneth.

KENNETH

I've got a brilliant idea. Instead of going on down the coast, this town is really the prettiest I've seen. Let's try to rent a house by the ocean. After we're through dinner, I'll look for a realtor and see if we can get something right down on the beach.

JAN

Oh, so that's why you bought me beach clothing.

KENNETH

Yep. Is there a real estate agent in town? (to the waitress)

WAITRESS

Oh there's several. The closest one is four blocks north on Shore Street.

KENNETH

Thanks and we're ready for lobster now.

[Scene of Jan and Kenneth walking back to their motel]

44. INT/ MOTEL ROOM—DAY

KENNETH

If we find a place to rent, then I'll rent a truck.

45. EXT/ TOWN SIDEWALK—DAY

Kenneth and Jan begin walking to the real estate office enjoying the sunny morning and the smell of salt air from the ocean.

46. INT/ REAL ESTATE OFFICE—DAY

Jan and Kenneth enter the real estate office as a bell sounds their entrance. A voice from the back yells that he will be with them in a minute. Kenneth picks up a copy of the local paper and notices an article on the second page about a missing girl from a Baltimore foster home.

KENNETH

Good afternoon. This is my niece Jan. My name is Kenneth Farnsworth. We're looking for a rental by the ocean.

REALTOR

We have quite a few places near the ocean but not right on the beach. Oh, I remember one older two story place in Edisto Beach.

But I don't think you would want that. How long were you intending to stay?

KENNETH

Possibly six months or longer.

REALTOR

That old farm house is cheap but it requires a full year's lease and you would need practically everything from an electric generator to some new bedding. But it is right on the ocean-maybe ten or twenty yards from the beach and it's quite secluded. Your nearest neighbor is almost out of site. If you're interested, I can take you out to see the place.

KENNETH

Let's take a look. O.K.? (To Jan)

Mind if I read your local paper on the way out? (To the realtor).

REALTOR

Go right ahead. There's a copy over on that side table.

Kenneth reads the article he had noticed about a runaway on the ride out to the beach house.

KENNETH (to himself)

This may be the perfect place for Jan who probably is the girl that has escaped. She apparently does not wish to return to that foster home, if she has gone to this much effort to get away.

47. EXT/ OLD HOUSE—DAY

[About 25 minutes later]

[Scene of realtor's car arriving]

The realtor stops in front of an old two story weather-beaten house.

[Scene of them walking out to the old house]

REALTOR

Notice the windows are all like this one, solidly meshing with the frame. Quite necessary for an ocean frontage place. But it will need a lot of things. Let's go around to the back door and immediately check the only water which is in the bathroom.

48. INT/ OLD HOUSE—DAY

Kenneth turns on the sink water facet and after a few bangs of the water pipe it spurts out some rusty water.

REALTOR

I'm afraid you'll have to bring out your own water in some sort of a container. Kind of like camping out.

KENNETH

Pretty rough but we'll make out O.K. since its still fall. We'll have to bring in some supplies of propane heat and I notice the downstairs is a total dusty mess that we will probably not use anyway.

They wander around the downstairs. Then they pass up the stairs that is surprising strong and into a huge open room with high ceilings - there being no attic.

Well this is nicer. We'll live up here and go down for water. The bed mattress will have to be replaced but this sofa looks half way new.

REALTOR

You have a fantastic view of the ocean from this balcony.

They walk over to it and test its strength by jumping lightly on it and then return to the lower floor and out through the door towards the beach.

KENNETH

How far do the property lines go?

REALTOR

I don't know but it says in this document that it is on sixty acres. So you must have heck of a lot of land probably extending over to the only house you can see over there. I'll try to find the map for this place. You can imagine there has been little interest in this old place. So you can catch me out with most questions.

KENNETH (to Jan)

Let's take it. Jan you straighten up around here a bit. I need to get back in town and buy a few things and rent a truck to haul the stuff back before dark. I'll be back in about three hours. Flashlights, that will be one important item, matches, and some sort of propane camp stove, something to eat, blankets and a mattress for your bed. I'm sure I'll think of several million other things.

JAN

I'll be fine.

49. EXT/ REALTOR'S CAR—DAY

Kenneth returns to town, signs the lease papers on the house, [scenes of walking around the town and looking at used trucks in a lot and then finding something suitable] and rents a used pickup truck that will negotiate the coastal road to the house. He buys a mattress, bedding, electric generator, wiring, propane gas stove, extra propane tanks, a small apartment type refrigerator and a variety of tools and groceries.

50. EXT. TRUCK—DAY

Darkness is beginning as Kenneth arrives back to the house. He sees Jan moving towards him in the yard.

JAN

You were gone longer than you said you would be. I was beginning to worry.

KENNETH

Sorry, but look what all I got. Help me up with the mattress.

[Scene: caring the mattress up stairs]

Tonight we'll have a mattress- burning party down at the beach with the old one.

51. EXT/ BEECH-NIGHT

Later that evening, exhausted from the afternoon's work, they just sit on the beach and watch the waves and the old mattress burn.

JAN

Let's make a small camp fire down here on the beach and cook some hamburgers for dinner.

KENNETH

And I bought some marshmallows just for such an occasion. So we'll roast some. I haven't done that since I was a kid.

[Cooking scene at the beach]

Kenneth puts his arm around Jan as night-time comes on and a general cool ocean breeze develops.

Are you warm enough?

JAN

For the moment, but I may want to turn my back to the fire and roast my other side. (To herself) I have never been so at peace in my life--thank you Uncle Kenneth.

KENNETH

I must reveal to you that I read an article in a newspaper I picked up in the real estate office about a girl running away from a foster home around Baltimore. It's alright, I'm sure you have your reasons.

Jan sleeps in the bed on the raised portion of the top floor and Kenneth uses the sofa in the middle of the room. Jan and Kenneth continue to develop their nest and the platonic relationship goes smoothly for months [scenes]. They walk the beaches periodically and enjoy each other's company --never a harsh word or argument.

FADE OUT

[LATER]

FADE IN

KENNETH

I've decided we're going to travel on down the coast to the to the Florida beaches for a vacation. You will comingle with the college gang that will be flooding the beach scene and you'll be safely lost among them as regards to any authorities.

JAN

Are you sure about this? It's not just what I said about being with people my own age is it?

KENNETH

No, but you're so right about that and there is no reason we can't pull it off, especially if you're willing to sleep in a camper. I'll rent one so we won't have to check in and out of motels giving fake names.

JAN

When do we start?

KENNETH

Anytime you wish my dear niece.

52. EXT/FARM HOUSE-DAY

[Next day/scene]

I guess that's it or did we forget your teddy bear.

JAN

Very funny Uncle Kenneth.

[Scene] Jan and Kenneth's camper pull out of the drive and down the road until the curve. Then onto the highway through Osborn as they head south. Their first stop is at Palm Coast, Florida just north of Daytona where they pull into a trailer court near the beach. The next morning both dawn their beach ware and take off to the warming sands. Kenneth takes a small blanket with him.

KENNETH

I will buy one of those beach umbrellas over at that shop. It will get plenty hot later on. Let's see, a yellow one would be good so you can see where we are on the beach after you've had your way with the waves. Let me go get us a couple of hot dogs. Be back in a minute.

A young man approaches Jan.

YOUNG MAN

Are you alone? Want to go swimming with me?

JAN

Oh, I think so but you'll have to wait till my uncle returns and I have my hot dog. O.K.?

YOUNG MAN

I'll run up to the stand and get one too and join you.

KENNETH

Who was that?

JAN

Just one of my admirers. He is coming back in a minute. He wants to go swimming with me. No doubt I'll have to save him from the big waves.

KENNETH

Sure- swim. That's what we're here for.

YOUNG MAN

We're just going right out here sir.

KENNETH

No problem. Have fun. By the way, what's your name?

YOUNG MAN

Kenneth, Kenneth Aldridge.

KENNETH

That will be easy to remember.

YOUNG MAN

(To Jan) Can you go out with me tomorrow evening to a dance they're having down at 'The Shark'?

JAN

Sorry we plan to leave in the morning. But thank you for asking.

[Scene]

Jan and Kenneth return to the trailer in the early evening; have ham sandwiches and lemonade and are soon under the spell of the exhausting day-dead asleep. Upon awakening Jan suggest they head back in the morning.

KENNETH

O.K. with me.

[Scene]

The truck is going back north. Kenneth spots a tavern and pulls off the highway.

JAN

I can't go in there.

KENNETH

Let's see. Hi. Can my niece come in with me if she doesn't order any alcohol?

BARTENDER

O.K. But make sure she doesn't drink any of yours or anyone else's.

Jan is approached by three different guys to dance during some loud 'honky tonk' music.

> KENNETH (to himself)
>
> Well she seems to be having fun and certainly doesn't have any problem meeting boys.

[Scene]

They stay the night at a trailer court in the camper next to the tavern, leaving early in the morning.

53. EXT/TRUCK—DAY

> KENNETH
>
> You sure seemed to enjoy yourself last night with those guys.

> JAN
>
> Seemed is the big word.

> KENNETH
>
> You mean you didn't?

> JAN
>
> I guess I did a little, but they always were trying to impress me about themselves. They sure seemed to mind their 'Ps and Q's' when I introduced them to my Uncle Reverend Farnsworth.

Both laugh.

> KENNETH
>
> That was a touch. I thought it would just temper any "hanky panky'.

JAN

I think I like you even more when you ventured out to find me a boyfriend.

KENNETH

Now, now. We have a difficult relationship as it is.

JAN

Difficult relationship—therein lies the problem.

Jan quickly looks away from Kenneth out of her side of the window, as a tear develops.

[LATER]

Subtitle [Jan's seventeenth birthday]

54. EXT/ BALCONY—NIGHT

JAN

(In a soft voice) Uncle Kenneth will you come out here? I have something I want to say to you.

55. INT/ BIG ROOM—NIGHT

KENNETH

Just a minute. I want to make sure all the candles are out.

56. EXT/ BALCONY—NIGHT

Kenneth walks out onto the balcony with Jan. [The ocean view is just after the sun slips below the horizon and the ocean is very still. The breakers can hardly be heard.]

JAN

Uncle Kenneth I'm not going to call you Uncle Kenneth ever again because I'm in love with you Kenneth.

She places both arms around his neck and kisses him passionately.

KENNETH

I'm overwhelmed. I really didn't have any idea you felt this way. I will definitely be looking at you differently from now on. Thank you Jan for your love. Let's walk the beach. Only this time we'll hold hands.

57. EXT/ BEACH—NIGHT

KENNETH

(As they are walking the beach and looking out over the ocean)

I believe love is independent of time and age.

JAN

You have never kissed me.

Kenneth takes her head in his hands and caresses her hair and then holds her body close to his, brushing his lips along her eyebrows and then passes his lips onto each eyelid and then down her nose, over to each cheek before kissing her on the mouth deeply and for a long time.

JAN

I realize I've never really been kissed before. Whew!

They gaze into each other's eyes in the moonlight before getting up off the sandy area and begin slowly back to the house. The ocean waves are quietly breaking upon the shore.

58. INT. UPPER LIVING AREA—NIGHT

Kenneth notices that Jan more and more looks deeply into his eyes. Two nights later Jan comes down to Kenneth's sofa and slips beside him. Nothing happens but a warm embrace and a snuggle.

59. INT. HOUSE—DAY

KENNETH

Now that you're seventeen years old, you should be graduating soon from high school. We're going to have to start you to school somewhere.

JAN

No, no, please. I just can't I can't. I tell you I won't. I can't explain. Just please don't make me.

KENNETH

Alright then, we'll start lessons here at home. I have a degree in philosophy. I think I'll try some holistic approach and derive the total universe and the history of the earth including not only American and European but Asian and African-- past and modern. I will probably have to check out quite a few library books, myself.

JAN

What happened to art and science?

KENNETH

Oh, it will get included as it was done or discovered. We'll have a regular time each day and spend an hour until I think you're up to some High School level of general information. OK? There are tests offered that will allow you a High School diploma.

JAN

Sounds good to me. Thanks for offering this.

[Study and teaching scenes]

KENNETH

Since you've not registered anywhere, it's a wonder some truant officer wouldn't have been snooping around here. We need to make a plan.

JAN

What kind of plan?

KENNETH

I'm thinking if school district officials come around, you need to hide somewhere. And besides your stuff would give you away. I've got it. You're going to love living out of a box. Don't look so sad. People that travel a lot live out of suit cases all the time.

JAN

What do we do first?

KENNETH

Let's take a look down stairs where we could pull up two or three of the board planks that make up the floor and have them ready to be put back down after lowering in the box with your stuff. And to be real clever, I'll bang around on other boards as a distraction to make it more obvious on those planks that I have been doing work on them. I can tell them I've been doing some repair construction here and there.

JAN

But what about me?

KENNETH

That might be more difficult but maybe the same idea would work. Let's say upstairs somewhere. The walls are not insulated but they do have a big space between them.

JAN

I'm going to stand inside the wall?

KENNETH

Exactly, and we'll put some bottled water in there in case you're in there very long and you'll have to promise me not to get fat.

JAN

(laughing) I don't think I could ever get fat.

KENNETH

Let's go up and take a look.

They go upstairs and inspect a likely wall area near the balcony.

Get me a hammer down near the plastic water tank. Now let me pull one of these boards away enough to take a peak.

JAN

What are you going to do-nail me in an upright coffin alive?

KENNETH

That's right. I'll pound around again on some other boards over there in the back and make it obvious. Then maybe even put in a new board back there.

JAN

I'll suffocate.

KENNETH

Not in these walls. Besides the worst scenario would be that they have a search warrant and that they would look around for a girl and she's nowhere to be seen and they would next go outside and check out the woods in back; look up and down the beach and then leave. Sorry about this but if we're going to beat the system we need some plan like this one. We'll try it out in a few days because we need a short drill to see how fast we can do things.

JAN

If I see a suspicious car approaching we'll go into action.

KENNETH

That's the spirit. Even if it is no one important, we'll be able to determine how good our plan works.

[Later]

JAN

Here comes a car!

They spring into their plan of action.

KENNETH

Well I'll be darned. Nearly two years and nothing and now suddenly –help me with the box. You've got everything in it that might give you away?

JAN

It's all there-let's time it.

KENNETH

Good ideal. OK. I got the time.

Kenneth nails down the boards over the box and takes the hammer upstairs with him. Then pries open the boards near the balcony and pounds it back after Jan slips inside. Someone knocks on the front door.

KENNETH

May I help you?

SALESMAN

I'm just covering the area and noticed this farmhouse. I represent the Washington Insurance Agency.

KENNETH

I assume this is life insurance. I already have life insurance, but appreciate your stopping by.

SALESMAN

Are there other members of this household I should be speaking with.

KENNETH

No, I live alone.

SALESMAN

Well thanks for chatty with me. Have a good day.

As the car goes back down the road, Kenneth rushes to pry open the board.

JAN

That wasn't too bad. Who was it?

KENNETH

Some insurance agent. But I'm afraid it will take longer if school officials come visiting.

JAN

How long did we take?

KENNETH

We took about two minutes which seems good enough to me. Let's not worry about it anymore. Do we have something for dinner this evening or do I need to look for 'road kill'?

JAN

Stop that. That's terrible. Help me return my box from downstairs.

60. EXT/ OLD HOUSE—DAY

[Scene]

[Fall]

Jan and Kenneth are chasing each other around the house. Jan is caught and screams with glee. Jan teasingly throws a bunch of leaves from Kenneth's basket into the air over in his area, so he has to re-rake.

KENNETH

You beast!

Kenneth then takes Jan's basket of leaves and tosses them into the wind. They struggle together. Then they fall to the ground face to face. Kenneth, pinning both arms against the ground, looks into Jan's eyes and their lips come very close. Then Kenneth jerks himself up.

[Scene]

[Winter]

Jan sneaks up to the back of Kenneth as he is shoveling and places a handful of snow down the back of his neck. Kenneth quickly bends over attempting to dislodge the snow and at the same time grabs Jan's ankle pulling her into a nearby snow bank.

[Scene]

[Spring]

Jan and Kenneth are planting tulip bulbs on the non-ocean side of the house. Jan begins to giggle.

KENNETH

What's so funny?

JAN

Nothing.

KENNETH

Come on now. Tell me.

JAN

But I'm telling you the truth. It's nothing—except that I'm so happy and I don't know why.

[Scene]

[Summer]

Jan and Kenneth are lying in a hammock together.

KENNETH

There that's the sound of some bird that I don't recognize. Can you see him?

JAN

Don't bother me. I'm watching a cloud change into something.

61 INT/FARM HOUSE—DAY

[Two weeks before Jan's eighteenth birthday]

KENNETH

There are two cars and they look kind of official with printing on the side. Isn't that a South Carolina logo. Action!

JAN

The box is ready.

KENNETH

There that does it for the box, but there's no time to get you in upstairs. Go through the back, through the woods.

Three school officials approach the front door.

KENNETH

Good afternoon gentlemen. How may I be of service?

OFFICIAL NUMBER ONE

We have been told by some town's people that you are living with a young girl out here. We would like to check on this because if the girl is of school age there could be serious charges made.

OFFICIAL NUMBER TWO

We have a search warrant to inspect the property.

KENNETH

(Almost saying 'we') waa…I don't live on the first floor. So you may find it a bit dusty. Not that you'll find the top floor immaculate either.

Kenneth notices them looking at the new wall board.

I've done the odd repair job to this house.

They also notice the extensive hammered area.

OFFICIAL NUMBER TWO

What's this about?

KENNETH

I have had squirrels infesting the place and I tried to scare them out of there. They get into the walls especially in the fall.

The men go upstairs and they look particularly at the camp stove and remaining area of the table.

Gentlemen, that's my kitchen you're in—in case you didn't realize it.

Again they gathered at the upstairs hammered area.

OFFICIAL NUMBER TWO

You two go check out that wooded patch in the back. I'm going down to the beach.

Next they come to the front door and say their goodbyes appearing to be satisfied that there was no girl about the premises nor evidence of one having been around.

[Two days later]

62. INT/FARM HOUSE—DAY

KENNETH (to Jan)

Here comes a car again today. I'll bet it's that housing inspector so you'll have to try and make it to the woods and then on down to the rocks because if it is the housing inspector he will be going over everything thoroughly. So cover yourself with seaweed. I'll try to keep them away from the back area. I'll come and get you—go!

Jan runs out the back door as Kenneth returns her luggage to the place on the first floor, covering it with the small rug.

63. EXT/FARM HOUSE—DAY

Jake Wilson, the county housing inspector, arrives with his assistant.

JAKE (as his car comes to the farm house, to his assistant)

After we meet Mr. Farnsworth, we'll go over the foundation first.

(To Kenneth)

Ah, Mr. Farnsworth. I didn't get an opportunity to go over the house carefully and check on county housing rules. If you'll permit my assistant and I inside your house we would appreciate it. I did notice several violations, two days ago on our first visit, when I was with the school officials. We're going to check the foundation first.

KENNETH

Sure, whatever you need to do.

64. INT/FARM HOUSE—DAY

JAKE

More squirrels?

KENNETH

More squirrels. (Checking his watch, realizing the tide was coming in.)

JAKE

I notice you look at your watch a great deal. Expecting guests?

KENNETH

No. No, take your time.

65. INT/FARM HOUSE—DAY

Jake soon returns to the open door and heads to the first floor with his assistant.

JAKE (to his assistant)

Go out to the truck and get me a crowbar and flashlight. I want to pull out some of these boards next to the new ones Farnsworth put in.

Finding nothing suspicious, Jake returns to the stairs and climbs to the second floor and does the same to the new boarded area.

KENNETH

I assume you will repair these areas?

JAKE

Maybe. I notice you have a camp stove in this —do you call it a kitchen area?

KENNETH

Yes

JAKE

That is against the fire code. What's this on the floor by your bedside? Have you taken to wearing lipstick?

Jake picks up Jan's lipstick she has neglected to put in the suitcase.

KENNETH (calmly)

That must belong to the gal I brought home last night from the Jefferson Club. Don't tell me there's a rule about not having sex in the housing code.

JAKE (flustered)

Very funny Mr. Farnsworth. See if you think this is funny. You have many violations and I will insist that you vacate these premises within three days or face eviction. Good day to you sir.

66. EXT/CAR—DAY

Jake and his assistant begin driving away.

[A few moments later as they are driving down the road]

ASSISTANT

I'd swear I saw a young girl back in the woods heading towards the beach when I was checking the foundation in the back.

JAKE

What? You stupid fool. That's where Farnsworth is hiding that girl. Well it's up to the school officials to take care of that matter anyway. So it's just as well that we didn't get involved. But I will tell them about this lipstick that I forgot, ha ha, to give back to Farnsworth.

67. INT/FARM HOUSE—DAY

As soon as they are gone, Kenneth frantically runs towards the big rock pile and begins screaming for Jan. As he nears the big rocks, he notices a figure clinging to one of the far out rocks. He realizes his worst fear. He splashes frantically continuing to call to Jan.

KENNETH

(Seeing a dark figure clinging to the outer rock)

Hang on! Hang on!

By the time he reaches her and wades back to the beach, she seems barely alive. He sits her down on the sand momentarily from the crashing waves and catches his own breath and regains a moment of strength. Then he pushes on her chest a few times and lifts her once more to his body. Her wet red hair covers the left side of her face.

(To himself) She is so cold.

Holding her tightly to his chest, he whispers in her ear.

> Stay with me. Don't leave me. I don't know what I'd do without
> you. I realize at this moment how much I love you Jan. Yes, I love
> you as you love me.

He takes her up the steps and wraps her in a blanket. Then returns to the leeward side of the house and begins taking out dry wood from the shed. Soon he has a good fire started. He races back up to Jan and carries her down the steps to the fire that warms her. She opens her eyes and whispers something. Kenneth cannot understand her. It is too feeble. Her body begins to warm more and Kenneth then thanks God for her life. Several hours later Jan becomes conscious and aware of things and looks at Kenneth.

JAN

I almost goofed. Didn't I?

KENNETH

Don't try to talk. I'm going to get you into your bed now.

Over the next few days Jan recovers and gains her strength in a rather remarkable fashion and begins toddling about with Kenneth watching intently. The crisis is over.

[later]

Kenneth serves Jan's eighteenth birthday cake and then pronounces that he is taking her to New York City to see a play as a gift. Jan is overcome with delight. She has never seen a live performance. Kenneth calls Barney, his agent, and has him arrange the New York trip. He also calls his lawyer in New York and makes an appointment to see him when they arrive. The next morning they head off to the commuter airport.

[Traveling scene and airport parking]

Jan has her first flight in a plane—a twin engine fourteen-seat prop type. At Miami they make their New York City connection and now it is Jan's first jet flight.

69. INT. MIAMI AIRPORT—DAY

JAN

Just thrilling, I had no idea. (To Kenneth)

The flight is over too soon. (To herself)

70. EXT/ NEW YORK CITY—DAY

KENNETH

I have to see my lawyer for a moment (to Jan as they enter a cab). Cabbie, take us to the 15th street building. (To Jan) I have an appointment at 11 AM. So let me introduce you to him and then if you wait in the sitting room, I'll be through my business in a few minutes.

71. INT/ LAW OFFICE—DAY

KENNETH

Hi Ted. This is Jan my girlfriend. Thanks for sending me the cash. I was quasi-incognito down in a little town.

TED

It's great seeing you again. It has been a long time. What have you been up to?

Jan steps outside of the office.

KENNETH

What this is all about will shock you. I love this young girl. I don't think she knows it yet. She has already fallen in love with me. She's a foster child and has been on the run, for two and a half years. This is the reason we are living in an old house by the ocean near a very small town in South Carolina. Now what I need is her real name. She tells me she never has given her real name or where her parents live to the foster parents. I intend to marry her. So in order to legalize any papers, I'll need that legal name and when and where she was born. She says she is eighteen. I don't care if you have to obtain this information by using illegal means. I need that name and whatever else is needed for the Virgin Island certificate. O.K.? Whatever the cost Ted. I'm desperate.

Kenneth goes out of the office saying goodbye to Ted and meets with Jan.

72. EXT /STREET—DAY

They proceed to a taxi and then into a theater where Kenneth's play is being performed.

73. EXT/THEATER—DAY

Upon arrival Kenneth goes up to the ticket window to buy two tickets and the first floor manager happens to be discussing something with the ticket girl. He notices Kenneth.

FIRST FLOOR MANAGER

Aren't you Kenneth Farnsworth?

KENNETH

Yes, but can't I by two tickets to my own play?

FIRST FLOOR MANAGER

Oh my God!

He quickly grabs the house phone

> Mr. Henry, guess who's down here? It's Kenneth Farnsworth, the playwright. Yes, he wants two tickets for tonight's performance. You say you'll be right down? I'll tell him to wait. (to Kenneth) Mr. Henry, the head of the theater, is coming down to meet with you Mr. Farnsworth.

JAN

> (To Kenneth) You're a playwright with a play on Broadway?

KENNETH

> Well, I have to earn money somehow to pay for all your beach clothes. (To Jan facetiously)

A moment later Mr. Henry arrives.

> This is Jan. She has never seen a play before. (To Mr. Henry)

MR. HENRY

> It's a pleasure to meet you. As you well know Mr. Farnsworth your play opened about three years ago at the Hobart Theater. When it closed two years ago I decided I would produce it here at our theater about a year ago. With less expensive tickets, compared to the Hobart Theater, we have been quite successful with your play. Let us get you private center seating in front sir.

74. INT/ THEATER—DAY

They arrive at the seats.

> I hope these will be satisfactory Mr. Farnsworth.

Jan is stunned by all the fuss that Kenneth is receiving but doesn't say anything more until Mr. Henry leaves. Kenneth removes Jan's coat.

Can you see the stage alright?

JAN

Oh, it's fine.

The play is almost ready to start when Mr. Henry appears center stage through the curtains.

MR. HENRY

We are fortunate tonight to have with us Mr. Kenneth Farnsworth,
the playwright of tonight's play, 'She and I Make Three'.

A blinding spotlight swings over onto where Jan and Kenneth are seated. There is a burst of applause as people stand up from their seats and turn to see Kenneth.

KENNETH (loudly)

You'd better see the play first before such an applause, but thank
you very much.

Jan is beside herself with questions and admiration for Kenneth.

Yes, I wrote this play and it has been doing well here on Broadway.

Jan tries to settle herself down as the orchestra begins to play. Kenneth observes Jan from time to time during the play from the corner of his eye and notices at times her pure delight. Then at one moment she grabs Kenneth's hand tightly and finally tears flow over her checks. She sits halfway forward in her chair as if not to miss a thing. Kenneth could not be happier for her.

75. INT/ RESTURANT—NIGHT

After the play, [scene shows them walking out onto the foyer of the theater] Kenneth and Jan have a full four course dinner at an Argentinean restaurant [scene] before checking into the airport for a night flight to Miami. [Scene] Kenneth calls Burney [scene] from his cell phone and asks if everything is arranged.

76. INT/ PLANE—NIGHT

                              JAN

What is arranged?

                            KENNETH

Oh a surprise party for you.

                              JAN

How can it be a surprise, now that I have heard you?

                            KENNETH

You'll see.

77. INT/ MIAMI AIRPORT—DAY [scene]

78. EXT/ VIRGIN ISLAND AIRPORT—DAY

Jan and Kenneth meet Burney at the airport and quickly switch to a commuter plane to the Virgin Islands.

                              JAN

What in the world is going on?

They meet another man driving an open jeep at the Virgin Island airport, riding through a bumpy jungle road to a beach cottage.

Where are you taking me Kenneth?

79. EXT/ BEACH HOUSE—DAY

KENNETH

You'll see. It will be the final phase of your birthday party.

They arrive at a rather modest beach house slightly elevated over a huge beach area. [Scene] Three fires about twenty-five yards apart are flaming and a native boy is going back and forth between the spits turning them. [Scene] Each spit has a whole pig on it, being slowly roasted over a bed of coals. [Scene] Soon people are arriving by the returning jeep, four or five at a time.

[Scene] Finally, there are around 35 friends, producers, directors, playwrights and other friends of Kenneth's at the beach. The beach party goes into full swing. There is a great deal of drinking and loud talking. [Scene]

KENNETH

Can I have everyone's attention please? Let's have a wedding. Jan come over here with me. Someone get some semi-dry kelp and let's make a wedding crown for Jan. Now all of you gather to form an aisle. We need a preacher. You look like a preacher—no wait a minute you be the preacher. Now who else do we need? Oh, let's make it realistic. Get some paper and act like these are formal documents that are required.

A MAN IN THE CROWD

Hey, I got some actual forms in my glove compartment. These are copies that my friend had, who got married two weeks ago.

THE SUPPOSED JUDGE (to Kenneth)

Sign these. You too Jan. Put down your real name dear. I won't show Kenneth and let's get this marriage going.

JAN

Such fun!

Kenneth and Jan stood at the end of the isle and soon the wedding march is being chanted by the crowd.[scene]

A MINISTER

Dearly beloved…Now I pronounce you husband and wife. You may kiss the bride. [Scene]

Everyone is half 'plastered' as they return to the cooking pigs and begin carving off large hunks, being washed down with jugs of wine. Jan begins to comingle with the guests.[scene]

GUEST #1

So you are now Mrs. Farnsworth.

JAN

Yeah. It feels great. Maybe someday I'll corner that man and really marry him.

GUEST #2

But I understand you are really married.

JAN

That can't be because I never even told Kenneth my real name.

Jan saunters over to another roasting pig and another group of guests.

GUEST

I think your Mrs. Farnsworth now, my lady.

Kenneth, Burney, and the preacher are on the beach house deck.

KENNETH

I think there may be about six people out there that know that Jan is really married. Look! There's an argument breaking out over there where Jan is.

Jan runs towards Kenneth.

JAN (To herself)

I'm going to put a stop to this nonsense.

As Jan approaches Kenneth,

KENNETH

Well, if it isn't Mrs. Farnsworth...

JAN

Kenneth stop that. I can't be married but three people insist that I am truly married to you. How can it be? Can that be true?

KENNETH

Don't you want to be married to me?

JAN

Of course, but...

KENNETH

That was a real minister, and those were real forms for marriage information and signatures required by the Virgin Island authorities. My lawyer researched your real name—Patricia Wilson. But you'll always be Jan to me.

JAN

Oh Kenneth I can't believe this. I'm the happiest girl in the world.

She dashes back into the crowd shouting,

I'm Mrs. Farnsworth!, I'm Mrs. Farnsworth!

80. EXT/ BEACH—NIGHT

Soon everyone but Burney has left and Burney sets off a few rockets over the bay. Kenneth and Jan hold hands and watch the sky light up.

[Then silhouettes are all that is left. Only a white screen shows. There are fades in and out of the rocket scene just after sunset and what appears to be technical blips showing is the rocket—beach scene. Then a white ghostly fade in showing a white building appears faintly at first and then more prominently.]

81. EXT/ BUILDING AND LAWN—DAY

Soon a full permanent view of the white building stabilizes as a figure is walking towards the camera. It is Burney.

BURNEY

Hi, Kenneth. How are you feeling today? You know you look much better than Tuesday when I visited you.

KENNETH

Burney, you old rascal. Where's Jan?

BURNEY

You know perfectly well Kenneth. Now look you have to eventually realize that Jan is dead! Until you do, the doctors just can't help you. Do you understand that? I just got through talking with them. They all agree Kenneth you've just got to come to grips with the fact that Jan is dead. Think back to those moments.

KENNETH (with vagueness in his voice)

Jan is dead. Jan is dead? Yes, Jan is dead. Oh yes, I remember now. She was so cold so wet. I remember getting her off the rocks. Slippery kelp, her body slippery, cold I managed to get her to the cold dark sand. Her red hair matted over her face. Her body next to mine.

[Overlay previous scenes of the rocky beach with Kenneth holding Jan]

I couldn't seem to get her body to become warm again. I remember how blue grey her face was. I couldn't get her warm, Burney. I just couldn't. I realize now she must have died in my arms.

BURNEY

Right, Kenneth. Hang on to that thought, however painful it must be for you, then and only then can the doctors help you. I implore you Kenneth. Please, please.

FADE IN—

83. INT/COURT ROOM SCENE (Burney himself recalling)—DAY

A court room is full of people.

BAILIFF

All stand. The honorable Judge Christine Gibson presiding.

JUDGE

(Sitting herself down) Is the prosecuting attorney and the defending attorney with his client present and ready for the proceedings?

Larry Simpson, Kenneth's lawyer stands.

SIMPSON

Present your honor.

Jim Thorp, the prosecuting lawyer stands.

THORP

Present your honor.

JUDGE

This court is in session. The defendant is charged with the murder of one Patricia Wilson, here forth known as Jan. Can someone explain this to me?

SIMPSON

The defendant did not know her real name and she refused to tell him, so between the two of them they decided upon the name Jan.

JUDGE

Thank you counselor. Will the prosecuting attorney call his first witness?

THORP

I call Mrs. Hall to the witness chair.

BAILIFF

Do you promise to tell the truth and nothing but the truth so help you God?

HALL

I do.

THORP

Sometime on June of two years ago did the defendant enter your café?

HALL

It's not my café. I was simply the waitress there.

THORP

Alright, I'll readdress the question. Did you wait upon this man?

HALL

Yes.

THORP

Did Mr. Farnsworth meet Miss Wilson there?

HALL

He saw a man....

THORP

Just answer yes or no.

HALL

Yes.

THORP

Did you overhear any of their conversation?

HALL

Yes, he suggested that he would find a motel for both of them.

THORP

That will be all, thank you.

SIMPSON

So under what circumstances did Mr. Farnsworth meet with Miss Wilson?

HALL

He saw her talking with a man across the street from the café.

THORP

I contest this. What is so wrong with a person talking with another person and why should he have interfered?

SIMPSON

Your honor, I will bring forth the relevance of this questioning.

JUDGE

Proceed.

SIMPSON

Yes, continue.

HALL

I thought he looked like a pimp who had been around the café recently and so I interpreted Mr. Farnsworth's actions which was to leave his meal and go into the street saying something that attracted her away from this man.

SIMPSON

Thank you.

THORP

Do you have evidence this man was a pimp and can you identify this person?

HALL

No.

THORP

Then it was simply your assumption.

HALL

Yes, but…

THORP

That will be all Mrs. Hall.

JUDGE

Since Mr. Simpson has indicated that he does not with to cross examine this witness, you may call your next witness Mr. Thorp.

THORP

Will Mr. Iverson step forward? Now tell the jury what your impression of Mr. Farnsworth and his so called niece were.

SIMPSON

Your honor, I object. Since when are impressions allowed into evidence?

JUDGE

Sustained.

THORP

Let me rephrase the question. Did Mr. Farnsworth ask you for two motel rooms? We know the famous playwright could afford two.

IVERSON

No.

JUDGE

Your witness Mr. Simpson

SIMPSON

No questions your Honor.

JUDGE

Your next witness Mr. Thorp

THORP

I could call forth the sales lady at the woman's shop, the waiter at the Shell Fish restaurant, the hardware employee, but the totality of the matter becomes obvious. The same story emerges. Paid by cash to keep his identity secret and sneak away to the costal place with this under-aged girl. But before the prosecution rests its case, I wish to call Mr. Farnsworth to the stand to ascertain just what he did do to Miss Wilson.

BAILIFF

Mr. Kenneth Farnsworth to the stand.

Kenneth's lawyer helps him up and accompanies him forward.

Do you promise to tell the truth and the whole truth so help you God?

KENNETH

Uhhh ahh

JUDGE

Please answer the question.

KENNETH

(as if attempting to answer) ahhh...ahh...

JUDGE

Will the defendant answer the question or I will have to hold you in contempt of this court.

KENNETH

Ahh....ah...ahh

JUDGE

Counselors please approach the bench.

Mumbling goes on between the three. The two counselors retreat to their seats.

I hereby dismiss today's court proceedings in order to obtain a mental evaluation of the defendant. Court will reconvene in two days. Court dismissed.

Two days later the court has reconvened and summaries have been requested.

SIMPSON

In summary we have a lonely man whose wife recently passed. He next befriended a person who happened to be a runaway foster child. Kenneth Farnsworth did not know she was being searched for nor did he harm her in anyway, unless giving food, clothing, and shelter is considered harmful these days. Yes he took her out of society's prying eyes because of the age difference and people's gossiping ways. He even did and structured home school for her. Hiding her from truant officers was really her desire not to go to school because she knew she be discovered as a runaway and returned to orphanage life that she had managed to escape from. Mr. Farnsworth did not kill Patricia Wilson, alias Jan. In fact he risked his life to save Jan from the rising tides. He is not an evil murder as the prosecution would have you believe. Save this kindly man.

JUDGE

Mr. Thorp please.

THORP

In summary, we have here an older man with lascivious thought and lecherous behavior. Mr. Farnsworth willfully attempted to hide his affair with this young girl, not even allowing her freedom to associate with persons of her own age and virtually holding her as a prisoner. To put it bluntly, he 'shacked' with a girl who was not only under-aged, but who was naïve, innocent and lacking intuitive judgment. There is no evidence that she drowned accidently. In fact, there is plenty of evidence to the contrary in that he had all the reasons in the world to silence his elicit affair with the young girl. How embarrassing it would have been for the great playwright if the affair was ever revealed. You, the jury, must put a stop to this man or he will simply repeat his actions in our society. Another victim will soon occur by the hands of this maniac.

JUDGE

The jury will retire and be it instructed that a unanimous conclusion is required by law for first degree murder.

Four hours later the jury enters the court room.

Who among you represents the jury? Sir, has the jury concluded with their decision?

JUROR

Yes we have your honor.

JUDGE

Would the Bailiff bring me their verdict? Will the defendant rise. You have been found guilty of first degree murder. In the light of this medical report I now hold in my hand, I am sentencing you to life imprisonment at the Dane County Asylum for the Criminally Insane.

Kenneth does not respond facially in any way. Barney has both hands in a tight fist on his forehead and appears to be in agony.

FADE IN

84. EXT/HOSPITAL LAWN—DAY

KENNETH

Yes, yes I can make it. I will. I will. Thanks Burney. You're all that I have left.

BURNEY

I've got to go now but I'll be back in a few days to see you again.

Burney turns and starts walking away from Kenneth—Burney waving as his back is to Kenneth.

KENNETH

Be sure and bring Jan with you next time.

Burney doesn't turn. He just keeps walking towards the building as tears roll over his face (close up).

END

II

WHAT'S IN A NAME

Registration # 1467612

Introduction

This is a teleplay and is approximately 45 min. long allowing 15 min. for advertisements.

FI

1. INT/ CROWDED RESTAURANT—DAY

> MR. CURRY

Is this seat taken?

> DR. JOHNS

No. Have a seat. This place is really crowded today. My name is Duncan and yours?

> MR. CURRY

Bill. I don't think I've seen you here before.

> DR. JOHNS

Well I'm a psychiatrist and many times I don't have time for lunch.

MR. CURRY

A psychiatrist! You may be just the man I desperately need, If you don't mind talking business.

DR. JOHNS

No. Go right ahead. That's what I'm for.

MR. CURRY (to the waiter)

I'll have a beef sandwich on rye and some ice tea, thanks. Well I have a twenty-eight year old daughter who has a problem of sever nightmares. I say sever because she has them practically every night.

DR. JOHNS

She lives with you?

MR. CURRY

Yes, she has lived at my house for a short time now. Hey, I'm having a small party and I could invite you along with the others; that away no one would suspect anything about your being there as a psychiatrist.

DR. JOHNS

Sounds fine. Here is my card. Call me anytime.

2. INT/ONGOING COCKTAIL PARTY—NIGHT

MR. CURRY (to Dr. Johns)

Glad you could make it. By the way, she's the one in the corner.

DR. JOHNS

Thanks. I'm sure things will be fine.

Dr. Johns begins introducing himself to some of the guests and purposely goes diagonally towards Christine and on arriving…

Hi. I see you're not exactly enjoying the party.

CHRISTINE

No, I just find my magazines as interesting as most of the guests and I don't drink much.

DR. JOHNS

I'm Duncan Johns and you are…?

CHRISTINE

Christine Curry

DR. JOHNS

Oh I see. Your Dad is the one that is doing the party. (Pause) I'll leave you alone I don't want to interrupt your reading.

CHRISTINE

I'm sorry. I didn't mean to imply such. It's just my way of protecting myself. I guess I'm really not too sociable.

DR. JOHNS

I find you to be as conversational as most, maybe perhaps a bit introverted. You see I'm a psychiatrist so I'm prone to analyze people constantly-sorry about that.

CHRISTINE

Oh that's O.K. I don't mind. I'm even a little flattered you would take the moment to analyze me.

DR. JOHNS

Well it was nice meeting you. I can never say to people hope to see you again for fear they will think I'm looking for business. Actually, I wouldn't mind seeing you again.

CHRISTINE

(Putting her magazine down and standing up)

Thanks for talking with me.

FO

FI

3. INT/MR. CURRY'S HOUSE—BEDROOM—NIGHT

Mr. Curry walks down the second floor hallway past Christine's bedroom and hears Christine screaming.

MR. CURRY

(Entering bedroom)

Wake up hon. Wake up!

CHRISTINE

What?

MR. CURRY

You were having one of your nightmares again. Do me a favor. You remember meeting one of my friends tonight at the party-a Dr. Johns, don't you?

CHRISTINE

Yes. He was very nice.

MR. CURRY

Why don't you see him sometime? Maybe he could help you.

CHRISTINE

I'll think about it.

4. INT/DR. JOHNS OUTER OFFICE—DAY

CHRISTINE

I'm Christine Curry I called earlier about an appointment to see Dr. Johns. I'm afraid I'm a bit early.

JOSEHINE (secretary)

Oh, you're fine. I'll tell him you're here.

[A moment later}

You may go in now.

CHRISTINE

Thanks

5. INT/DR. JOHNS INNER OFFICE—DAY

DR. JOHNS

Well, I guess I do get to see you again. Sit right over here. Let's see now. You told Josephine that you're having recurrent nightmares-right?

CHRISTINE

Yes, I've had them for years. I'm really quite use to them, if you can ever get use to nightmares.

DR. JOHNS

I need to ask you quite a few personal questions but it will get easier after we get to know each other. I hope that's alright with you.

CHRISTINE

Oh, yes. We've had our moments but nothing serious.

DR. JOHNS

What about your mother?

CHRISTINE

What about her?

DR. JOHNS

Well I know from knowing your father that he is separated. What can you add?

CHRISTINE

Not very much.

DR. JOHNS

Have you ever thought about hypnotism? Is it something you would try? And if so, will you allow me to hypnotize you on our next visit?

CHRISTINE

You can hypnotize me now, if you think it might help.

DR. JOHNS

Fine. I want you to move over on this couch and let me pull the blinds. Now all you have to do is relax and look at this small flashlight as I move it slowly in front of you. Don't think about anything and if you wish you can just go to sleep.

A few moments later Christine is in a hypnotic state.

Christine can you hear me?

CHRISTINE

Yes.

DR. JOHNS

Christine tell me about your mother when you were young. Was she nice to you? Do you like your mother? This is Dr Johns. Talk to me it's all right.

CHRISTINE

I hate her! I hate her!

Christine begins to cry and tighten her fists and pounds on the sofa.

DR. JOHNS

Listen to me Christine. Tell me why you hate her.

CHRISTINE

I hate my mother.

DR. JOHNS

When I say five you will wake up and you will not remember any of this. One, two, three, four, five.

CHRISTINE

What happened?

DR. JOHNS

You were under hypnosis. I was learning about your relationship with your Mother.

CHRISTINE

What did you learn?

DR. JOHNS

Christine, I really need to go over my notes and then we can go over it next time. If you want so see me again.

CHRISTINE

Let me think about all of this.

[The next week]

6. INT/DR. JOHNS' OFFICE—DAY

DR. JOHNS

Here we are again. How have things been?

CHRISTINE

Oh, about the same. I have had three nightmares since I saw you.

DR. JOHNS

What are they about?

CHRISTINE

They always seem to involve a doll.

DR. JOHNS

Let's put you under hypnosis and see what we can learn about dolls.

CHRISTINE

O.K. I want to know more of what you have learned about Mother.

DR. JOHNS

The dolls may be connected to your feelings about your Mother.

Soon Christine is in a hypnotic state.

Tell me Christine about dolls in your childhood. Did you like to play with dolls? Did you have a particular doll you liked?

CHRISTINE

No. I hate dolls! I'm scared of dolls!--especially the doll beside me.

DR. JOHNS

What doll is that?

CHRISTINE

The one that I always find when I wake up in the middle of the night,--that doll, that one there.

Christine screams.

DR. JOHNS

Tell me about the doll. Does it have rouge on the cheeks?

CHRISTINE

No,

DR. JOHNS

Does it have a smile?

CHRISTINE

No.

DR. JOHNS

Are the eyes blue or brown?

CHRISTINE

No.

DR. JOHNS

Does it have a nose?

CHRISTINE

No.

DR. JOHNS

Doesn't it have any kind of face?

CHRISTINE

No.

DR. JOHNS

I see. It's a faceless doll!

FO

FI

7. INT/DR.JOHNS' OFFICE—DAY

DR. JOHNS

Christine this is your third visit and I will once again put you in hypnosis. I can tell you we are making great gains and I think soon I will be able to tell you what is causing your nightmares.

Christine is under hypnosis.

DR. JOHNS

Christine when you go to bed does your mother put the faceless doll beside you?

CHRISTINE

I don't think so.

DR. JOHNS

When you wake up in the middle of the night is the faceless doll beside you?

CHRISTINE

Yes.

DR. JOHNS

Well then, who do you think put the doll beside you?

CHRISTINE

My Mother.

DR. JOHNS

How do you know that? You were asleep.

CHRISTINE

Because my mother thinks my father loves me more than her. My mother does not like me.

DR. JOHNS

Now Christine I want you to relax and come out of hypnosis.

[A moment later]

DR. JOHNS

Now that you are out of hypnosis, I can tell you something your conscious mind has suppressed.

First let me ask you 'Do you love your Mother?'

CHRISTINE

Of course, you're supposed to always love your mother.

DR. JOHNS

Not always.

CHRISTINE

Well.

DR. JOHNS

You are an exception. You do not love your mother. She had been frightening you for years when you were sleeping by placing a faceless doll in your bed and then removing it later before you awoke. She must have disliked you very much because this is a very cruel thing to do to a child. Upon your next appointment, without hypnosis, we're going to talk about your mother and father openly now that you know and understand this matter a little better.

F.O.

[Next week]

FI

8. INT/MR. CURRY'S HOUSE—NIGHT

CHRISTINE

Hi. Father. Thought I'd like to visit with you a while.

MR. CURRY

Glad you did. I've got a chance to ask you how it's going with Dr. Johns.

CHRISTINE (to herself)

(I don't want Father to know that Mother is the cause of my nightmares.)

Oh, things are going slow but he does seem to be helping me I appreciate your concern Father. Let me say this—I will try to tell you as much as I can without hurting either of you.

MR. CURRY

What do you mean?

CHRISTINE

Just that. Parents raise children. Sometimes they do things incorrectly. But let's have dinner together and forget these things for now

9. INT/DR. JOHNS' OFFCE—DAY

DR. JOHNS

Nice to see you again Christine. Now let's set down to he business of talking about your Mother and Father and how they got along.

CHRISTINE

I remember my father always arguing with my mother about my bangs. I still ware my bangs long to this day. It seems the right thing to do and frankly I know I'm not attractive so I feel more hidden by these long bangs. I remember a specific argument that father had one day.

[Flashback]

MR. CURRY

I'm furious with you Mildred for cutting Christine's bangs that long. You're making it purposely long because you are jealous of Christine's basic good looks.

CHRISTINE

Later that evening they were still at it. Father threatened to leave mother if she didn't stop berating me.

DR. JOHNS

Did he?

CHRISTINE

Eventually yes. Let me tell you about the house on Charlotte Street. It was lined with rows of tall elm trees. The entrance had a few steps leading to a front short hallway that led forward to the stairs to bedrooms above, my grandmother's place, a renter and my small apartment. At the bottom of the stairs to the left, upon entering, one would go down a step to a darkened living room with an unused fireplace covered with a picture screen. Above the fireplace hung a large blue-green landscape made by a previous renter. The blinds were always pulled. I remember an aquamarine enameled small metal fan slightly disturbing the hot humid air over a drunken woman, my Mother, whose saliva rolled out of side of her mouth –a mouth with a thick layer of lipstick. Empty beer cans litter the floor of the room next to the gloomy dark living room. There was always a heavily laden stench of beer. She drank only beer and her appearance became ugly. When I was eight, father became enraged when he found me drinking a can of beer. I remembered I rather enjoyed it because I would fall asleep in the afternoon easily and escape all the loud arguing. He told mother if she ever gave beer to me again he would have her arrested.

DR. JOHNS

Those must have been sad days for you Christina. I think that will be enough for today.

10. INT/DR. JOHNS' OFFICE—DAY

Christina let's just talk a little about you for a change. You must have been aware all those years as a young woman through magazines and ads, etc. that women become more attractive through dress and cosmetics.

CHRISTINE

I never had much money for a nice wardrobe and I didn't want to ask my father for money since he was a pensioner. I admit I never used much cosmetics because, I was afraid that I might attract some man and I wouldn't know how to handle myself or the situation; what to say, what to do. Actually I had a boyfriend one time when I worked at an office for a short time. He was the mailroom boy and we went to the movies on occasion.

DR. JOHNS

What happened to your job?

CHRISTINE

I was kind of an assistant secretary but the boss hired a good looking typist that became my immediate superior who soon fired me. Without cause I might add.

DR. JOHNS

Let's experiment a bit then with your looks. I will see how it affects your personality. OK? First begin using a bright red orange lipstick. When you are use to that get your hair styled, something that others would wear. Look at women your age when you walk down the street. Then make an appointment for two weeks from now and we'll have a talk then. By the way Christine, you told me one time under hypnosis about a place at the corner of Fourteenth Street and Fifth Avenue. What does that mean to you?

CHRISTINE

The address doesn't 'ring a bell'. I can't imagine.

DR. JOHNS

Well at our next meeting I want you to find out what's at that address and explain any relevance it may have for you.

F.O.

11. INT/RESTAURANT— DAY

F.I.

[Scene]

Gerald (Christine's older brother) and Christine are waiting for their lunch order.

GERALD

I know you don't like our Mother but after all she is our Mother and she needs us.

CHRISTINE

Who told you I don't like Mother. I love Mother the same as anyone else does.

GERALD

Well then why haven't you visited her in the past few years? That pretty well tells the story I think.

CHRISTINE

You've been away too.

GERALD

But I've seen her several times lately.

CHRISTINE

I am not as strong as you. I still have problems with a mother that drinks.

GERALD

Well you should go see her now and then like I do, you can take it for a few days at a time.

CHRISTINE

I don't think I could take it for a few hours.

[Scene]

They are served.

CHRISTINE

I don't think I ever told you that I tried to get Mother to stop drinking many times after you left home. I would get so frustrated of her buying beer and hiding it around the house that I would pound my head against the wall in the kitchen. One time I found five cans of beer and I poured them right in the middle of the rug in the front room and left them just to show Mother I knew what she was doing.

GERALD

I had no idea you went through those kinds of things. I always thought you just loved Mother and that was that.

CHRISTINE

I do, I do. But I had to live with all of her problems. I was so frustrated that eventually I too left her. How did you escape the problems I seemed to accumulate from my earlier days?

GERALD

You seem to forget I'm older than you and got on my own rather quickly. You remember I was offered that job at the newspaper when I was only seventeen.

CHRISTINE

I've always loved my family but I never expressed myself to Mother or Father. I was just too inward somehow.

GERALD

You were difficult to know Christine. But I always liked you. Don't be too hard on yourself.

CHRISTINE

But I'm loaded with regrets and I don't seem to have a life even now.

GERALD

You'll be fine—hang in there kid.

CHRISTINE

Why haven't you ever married Gerald?

GERALD

I wasn't going to tell Dad or you right now, but I'm engaged to a girl that I've only known for three months. I fell in love with her, just like that.

CHRISTINE

Fantastic Gerald! I am amazed. Congratulations. Where did you meet her?

GERALD

I was at a party of a friend of mine and she and I just hit it off. You'll get to meet her soon. She's from Georgia. Only one big problem with all of this, she has a St. Bernard pup. Where is it going to be during our honeymoon? Her parents live in a tiny apartment.

CHRISTINE

Bring it to Dad's place. It's a big house and they'll be friends in no time and I'll take care of it because I intend to move there soon.

GERALD

Not a bad idea. In fact that's great. That is so very kind of you Christine. Somehow we have never helped each other this way. Strange. (pause) I think you are the one that has changed.

CHRISTINE

What's next for all of us? Well, all but you—you're getting married. I feel sorry for Mother and Dad. Mother an alcoholic and Dad living by himself- well, until I show up. I guess this is life. I don't know. I don't understand. Are we a typical family? I think not. You be sure and stay in touch with me.

[Scene]

They kiss goodbye.

FI

[Flashback]

12. EXT/STREET CORNER—DAY

Christine goes into Tim's Tavern and checks the street sign it's Fourteenth Street and Fifth Avenue.

13. INT/TAVERN—DAY

BARTENDER

Good evening Christine. I have set up your brandy in the back corner table per usual.

CHRISTINE

Good evening Jake. Thanks

[Scene]

The clock passes through two hours. The bartender helps the drunken Christine into a taxi.

BARTENDER (to the taxi driver)

Be sure she enters the building where she lives.

14. EXT/APARTMENT BUILDING—DAY

[Scene]

Christine stumbles up the stairs leaving the key in the lock of her apartment and collapses onto the bed. Gerald Curry drops by Christine's apartment to make one of his rare visits.

15. INT/APARTMENT—NIGHT

Upon coming to the door he notices the key is in the door. Taking the key he enters the front room and puts the key on the table, then proceeds to the bedroom.

GERALD

Christine it's me, Gerald.

He shakes her several times and is about to call for an ambulance but then smells Christine's breath and realizes she is drunk.

(Loudly near her ear) Christine, who did this to you?

CHRISTINE (awakening slightly)

No one but me.

And then she falls back into a stupor.

GERALD (to himself)

I can hardly believe it.

Gerald closes the door leaving the key on the table. Then he knocks on the manager's door downstairs.

GERALD (to the manager lady)

I found my sister taking a nap. I didn't want to wake her—so would you mind locking the door? She had left it open and I don't have a key. Thanks. Don't tell her I was here. I'll see her later. Thanks.

Gerald leaves the apartment building.

F.O.

F.I.

16. INT/OFFICE—DAY

[Allison-Christina's office Colleague]

ALLISON

Hi. Welcome to the office gang. Where are you staying?

CHRISTINE

First let me say that I left my Father's house, which is out in Raleigh suburbs, when I got this job. I needed to be closer to the office so I'm now at The Hotel Clark but actually I'm looking for another spot because it's a little too shabby there.

ALLISON

Shabby? That's the least of it. It's dangerous down there. Listen, I've got an idea. How about splitting rent at my little apartment? It's big enough for the two of us. Let me put it this way, I'm very nice.

They both laugh.

CHRISTINE

That would be great.

ALLISON

Do you have a car?

CHRISTINE

No. I don't even know how to drive.

ALLISON

This Friday let's leave together after work and you stay over with me and Saturday morning we'll drive over and get your stuff and drag it back.

CHRISTINE

I don't have much and I only have two more days left in rent that I've paid for already.

ALLISON

I'm sure we'll get along fine, but you never know.

CHRISTINE

I'm sure we'll get along.

[Scene]

Christine working with Allison in an office.

CHRISTINE

Allison you always seem so bright and cheerful. I envy you. You must think I'm the driest person in the world.

ALLISON

No, not really. You just need to get out more.

CHRISTINE

But I have no one to go out with. If I go out alone, I would never know how to act.

ALLISON

All you need is confidence. I know, let me help you with your make up. Come on over here and we'll make magic.

CHRISTINE (afterwards)

My gosh! I do look different. What did you do to me?

ALLISON

You see that. That's all you needed. Next you'll be competing with me-you beast.

17. INT/WORK OFFICE—DAY

ALLISON (opening door to office supplies)

Sorry!

Allison quickly closes door. Christine and the office gopher Jack are kissing.

[Later]

ALLISON (to Christine)

I didn't mean to pry. Well it is surprising. Finally got a boyfriend, huh?

CHRISTINE

Stop your teasing. You know how romantic things are so difficult for me.

ALLISON

I think it's wonderful.

Allison leaves the office early on the pretext she is not feeling well.

18.INT/ALLISON'S APARTMENT—NIGHT

ALLISON (to herself)

I need to get ready for my early date tonight.

[Knock on door]

ALLISON

Who is it? (Opening the door slightly]

MARGO

Hello, my name is Margo. I'm Christine's sister. Is she home yet?

ALLISON

Come on in. Why no. She'll be home shortly. Have a seat. Somehow I don't recall Christine mentioning she had a sister. Do you live in town?

MARGO

Yes.

ALLISON

I'm sorry but I'm in a rush to get ready for my date tonight. Can I just ask you a quick question?

MARGO

Sure. Fire away.

ALLISON

Christine very seldom goes on dates. Do you two ever double date?

MARGO

No, we don't and now that Jack, my boyfriend and I are going steady I wouldn't especially start that sort of thing now.

ALLISON

That's quite an extraordinary coincidence.

MARGO

What's a coincidence?

ALLISON

The name Jack.

MARGO

What about Jack?

ALLISON

May I ask where he works?

MARGO

He works with you and Christine's at the office.

F.O.

F.I.

19. INT/BAR—NIGHT

[Scene]

Margo sits at the bar sipping a cocktail Dr. Johns sits beside her and strikes up a conversation.

DR. JOHNS

Hi.

MARGO

Hi.

DR. JOHNS

Come here often?

MARGO

No, just now and then and this is 'now'.

They both laugh,

DR. JOHNS

My name is (He hesitates) Mike and yours?

MARGO

Margo

DR. JOHNS

It is nice to meet you Margo.

MARGO

What kind of work do you do?

DR. JOHNS

That's a very good question. I don't know.

MARGO

That's alright you don't have to answer that.

DR. JOHNS

Oh, I think I'll have to leave (looking at his watch). It was great meeting you. Maybe we can meet here again sometime.

Dr. Johns leaves and catches a cab. Margo finishes her drink.

F.O.

F.I.

20. EXT/CAR—DAY

MARGO (looking out of her back-view mirror to herself)

There goes a perfectly fine shopping day.

POLICE OFFICER

Let me see your driver's license please. Do you realize how fast you were going Miss, Miss ah, Curry?

MARGO

No, I'm afraid I wasn't paying enough attention.

POLICE OFFICER

Well madam I'm going to have to give you a ticket. Let's see Christine Curry, number…

MARGO

My name is Margo Curry. Let me see that. Why this is my sister's license.

POLICE OFFICE

This photo I.D. looks like you.

MARGO

Well it isn't.

POLICE OFFICE

Well then I'll have to tack on a fine for not having your driver's license with you.

MARGO

Do what you have to do.

POLICE OFFICER

If I were you I'd scamper down at least tomorrow and pay this because it will compound every day after that. Good day.

MARGO (Driving away)

How in the hell did I end up with Christine's driver's license?

[Scenes]

Christine at Allison's marriage ceremony.

F.I.

21. INT/DR. JOHNS' APARTMENT—NIGHT

[Scene]

Dr. Johns enters his apartment and begins to fix his dinner.

DR. JOHNS (to himself)

I haven't already eaten have I? It seems that I know but maybe that was last night. If so I can't remember what it was that I had. Was I at a restaurant last night or this evening before coming home? I think I've been working to hard. I'll take some 'night-night' pills and go to bed early this evening.

[Scene]

Christine moving in at her father's house.

22. INT/MR. CURRY'S HOUSE—DAY

CHRISTINE (coming through doorway and entering with luggage)

Father this is awfully nice of you to let me stay with you.

MR. CURRY

Christine I would have it no other way. You know what it's like to live alone. It's darn miserable. Where're you going?

CHRISTINE

I've got to get more of my things out in the cab. Allison couldn't help me, she's being married, but I decided to call you and see if I could come out today. Glad you said yes. We've been apart too long.

MR. CURRY

You look a little different Christine. That office job is good for you I think.

CHRISTINE

I must say you look a little slower. Are you O.K.?

MR. CURRY

I'm doing fine. After all when you are hundred years old you slow down.

CHRISTINE

I hope this works out. Allison is going to pick me up from here to get to work.

MR. CURRY

I have noticed I can't get out of soft chairs that I can easily manage to get into. That's my primary gripe.

CHRISTINE

Now that I'm here, you can yell for me to help you.

MR. CURRY

Sit down over here. You can take those things upstairs later. Use my old room. It's big. So sit a spell. How's your love life?

CHRISTINE

That's the beginning of our conversation? To answer your poorly placed question, it's just like it was. I had one office 'boy friend' and that lasted a couple of weeks. I guess I need a face transplant.

MR. CURRY

You are a beautiful woman, so stop saying those things.

They both rise and embrace.

CHRISTINE

Oh, Father I'm so frightened.

MR. CURRY

Frightened of what?

CHRISTINE

I've always been frightened of other people. It's good that my work just keeps me in a cubby hole with a computer.

MR. CURRY

What does Doctor Johns say? You're still seeing him aren't you?

CHRISTINE

Oh, he says he is finding out why I'm so frightened in my sleep but he doesn't know yet why I'm frightened of people when I'm awake.

MR. CURRY

Sounds like great progress he's pretty good huh?

CHRISTINE

He's wonderful.

MR. CURRY

How wonderful?

CHRISTINE (blushing)

Very wonderful-but you'll be my favorite Father no matter what. In fact you're the only Father I've got. I love you Father and don't you forget it.

MR. CURRY

Thanks Christine.

F.O.

[Scene]

Gerald visits with his Father.

GERALD (to his Father)

Soon after you left Mother, I felt sorry for myself, alone and being the only male in the family and I was not friendly towards females, especially living with any of them and especially not with Mother in her condition, nor Christine who seemed lost in her life with no direction. It was not that I didn't love them; I simply didn't know what to do with them. Subconsciously, I realized I was abandoning Christine but believed her to be old enough to protect herself from her surrounding problems. I was wrong and I have great regrets now looking back on the situation. I have to live with these regrets now and forever.

MR. CURRY

Don't be so hard on yourself. You believed you were doing something right or at least something instead of squandering your life there in that house. If anyone should have regrets it is me-- the head of the household. I was saving my mind. I couldn't even think in terms of Christine and you. I simply had to go.

It has been a blessing with Christine's arrival and living with me. I only hope she finds a life for herself. She's terribly young still and needs a love life. She never seems to date or go out evenings to socialize. But she has spruced herself up recently and really is looking quite nice.

GERALD

I have to agree about that. All I can think about that is it about time she shows off her beauty. But I wonder why now. What started her change?

MR. CURRY

Oh, she hasn't told you. There is nothing to be ashamed of but she's been seeing a psychiatrist about a nightmare problem. He seems to really be helping her. She is even becoming more outgoing.

GERALD

What's his name?

MR. CURRY

Dr. Duncan Johns.

GERALD

I'd like to talk with him before I leave for home. Do you think that would be alright?

MR. CURRY

Sure. Why not? Maybe you can tell him something about Christine that would be helpful.

[Scene]

Margo shows up at the front door. Gerald is standing by the library door next to the hallway entrance and overhears some of the conversation between his Father and Christine. He is amazed at Christine calling herself Margo.

GERALD (To himself)

I have no idea about what to do now.

GERALD

Oh, hello.

MARGO

My name is Margo, I'm Christine's sister.

GERALD

I'm a friend -just a guest of Bill's. Glad to meet you but I'm in a bit of a hurry. Hope to see you again soon.

Gerald rushes to his car to see Dr. Johns.

23. INT/DR. JOHNS' OFFICE—DAY

GERALD (To Josephine)

I'd like to see Dr. Johns as soon as possible. It's a bit of an emergency.

JOSEPHINE

He's with another patient. I'll see if he can step out for a moment.

DR. JOHNS

Yes?

GERALD

I'm Christine's brother.

DR. JOHNS

How do you do? So your Christine's brother.

GERALD

I'm here because Christine's out at Father's house saying her name is Margo.

DR. JOHNS

I cannot discuss client information, but how did you handle that?

GERALD

I told her I was a friend of Bill Curry.

DR. JOHNS

That's about all you could have said. You did the right thing. Thanks for dropping by and telling me this.

GERALD

By the way, haven't I seen you before? You look very familiar.

DR. JOHNS

No. I don't think so.

GERALD

I'd swear I've met you. Yes, yes, you look exactly like Jason, a man I talked with at a restaurant bar two nights ago.

DR. JOHNS

Sorry, I guess we all have 'look a likes'. Now that I have the chance to ask you, can you remember Christine as a child having a faceless doll?

GERALD

No, I don't remember such a doll. Did she say she had one?

DR. JOHNS

I really shouldn't reveal what Christine said or didn't say but if you remember something about this call me from your home later.

GERALD

Yes. I will. Anything I can do to help.

24. INT/MR. CURRY'S HOUSE—DAY F.O.

[Scene]

Gerald drives back to his father's place.

GERALD

Father, what's going on with Christine?

MR. CURRY

I think she had just given herself a nickname- Margo.

GERALD

I think it's much more serious than that. I've just seen Dr. Johns and although he won't say anything, he indicated that he was treating her and I believe for more than just nightmares.

MR. CURRY

Here comes Christine now.

CHRISTINE

Hi, Big brother. What are you doing here, just visiting?

GERALD

Christine I want to talk to you. Let's go up to your room.

CHRISTINE (on the way up the stairs)

Sounds serious.

GERALD

It is.

Gerald enters Christine's room.,

CHRISTINE

Now what's so important?

GERALD

Christine I saw and heard you a few hours ago talking with father and telling him your name was Margo.

CHRISTINE

That is strange. Dr. Johns mistakenly called me Margo one time recently.

GERALD

You were wearing a short dress and looked somehow differently.

CHRISTINE

Well let's just see.

Christine opens up her clothes closet.

Here are my clothes. Oh, except for these two that I must have taken by mistake when I moved from Allison's apartment.

GERALD

There it is!—the yellow one. That's the one you were wearing. I must admit you looked rather cute in it.

CHRISTINE

Now is no time to jest.

Christine goes to Gerald and they embrace.

I'm frightened. What is happening?

25. INT/DR. JOHNS' OUTER OFFICE—DAY

Margo signs in at Dr. Johns' office. His secretary, Josephine, has stepped out of the office for a moment. Dr. Johns opens his office door and meets Margo, almost saying 'Hello, Christine', but notices she has signed in as Margo.

26. INT/DR. JOHNS' INNER OFFICE—DAY

DR. JOHNS

Please step in-- Miss Curry, I believe.

MARGO

Just call me Margo.

DR. JOHNS

My name is Dr. Johns. Just call me Dr. Johns.

Both laugh

DR. JOHNS

How may I help you?

(To himself) I can't believe what I'm seeing. It's Christine with a short skirt, bangs and the remaining hair tied back with pink ribbons, thick bright lipstick color, mascara with glitter, and dark eyeliner.

MARGO

My sister says she is seeing you because she is having nightmares and I thought I might help you in some way.

DR. JOHNS

Yes, but of course you can.

(To himself) I had no idea she has a multi-personality disorder just like her brother was trying to tell me.

MARGO

Christine is just unattractive, and if I may say so she has 'zilch sex life'. Now I have no boyfriends, just men and I have sex with all of them.

DR. JOHNS

May I ask do you drink a great deal, Margo?

MARGO

I have an occasional drink but no--no I don't drink a lot. I don't even like the stuff that well. Incidentally, Christine drinks heavily and usually at Tim's Tavern in the evenings. By the way, haven't I seen you before somewhere? I guess you just look something like Mike I met a few nights ago.

DR.JOHNS

I don't know who you could be talking about. I hope you won't think I'm too forward, but do me a favor and let me see if there is a change in the number of men in your life if you wear longer skirts and less makeup. Let's just consider it an experiment.

MARGO

Sounds like fun. When do I report the results of this experiment?

DR. JOHNS

Say in two weeks—yes, tell Josephine you want an appointment to see me in two weeks.

[Two weeks later]

27. INT/DR. JOHNS' OFFICE—DAY

JOSEPHINE

Dr. Johns, Miss Margo Curry to see you.

DR. JOHNS

Oh, how nice to see you and indeed how different you look. Well, tell me what happened to your dating list.

MARGO

I wouldn't have believed it, but there was no change. I guess I can save some money on makeup also.

DR. JOHNS (to himself)

They are beginning to dress similarly. Furthermore, I notice that Christine/Margo is quite attractive.

CHRIISTINE

You know I drink heavily at Tim's Tavern, but now I only drink occasionally. I can't understand what changed me. Did you do that somehow?

DR. JOHNS

I'll explain what is happening to you later. I don't dare tell you why you don't like drinking now. You wouldn't believe me anyhow. For example, you have a fantasy that you go out with scads of male companions and you have sex with all of them. Do you think that is true?

CHRISTINE

Dr. Johns, please.

DR. JOHNS

I didn't think so. As I said someday soon I'll explain all this.

28. INT/MR. CURRY'S HOUSE ENTRANCE—DAY

CHRISTINE

You know Father I feel that I don't even know you somehow. Of course you were gone from home for years, so it seems that just now I'm starting to get to know you better; and I might add you're a great, Father. I'm very tired and I'm going straight up to bed this evening. We'll chat together tomorrow. Goodnight.

[Dream sequence, sepia colored, somewhat blurry]

I'm falling, falling into a rocky crevice; my ankles hurt, the wind is becoming stronger and colder, I cannot stand, there are massive rocky peaks between vast distances, blue in a haze, wisps of high thin clouds, then heavy black ones amass above; rock surrounds me in every direction, yet I feel exposed as being on an open field; the pitch of the wind whistles; I feel myself panicking at my hopelessness; I search frantically at the steep ravine below dotted with myriads of small scrub brush; a yellowish sand bar rests in the canyon far below, curling back on itself momentarily and then disappearing around the base of a mountain; now I can see a figure scaling down the other side of the ravine; I follow it with fascination, a little later I lose sight of the figure which reappears at intervals; soon a man is climbing up just below me; as he comes into view I notice is face covered with a grey white beard; neither of us try to speak, he is like some wild beast prowling around me; he wraps a blanket from his backpack, throws it around me and mumbles in German and French to himself; he removes some rope from is gear and suddenly lifts me effortlessly onto his back; we begin to descend over the edge; I put my arms around his chest and I can feel his heart pounding through his jacket; now we are ascending a rocky slope to a cabin; it is beginning to snow; he looks into my eyes as if to evaluate me in some way; roar of wind; I see the cabin not far above us; the mountain is slowing his movements; I cling fiercely; I am facing his cabin that is wedged into a stone overhang; he stops, now the snow begins to accumulate on us; tears are going over both of his cheeks; he simply cannot move anymore; I drop myself down and drag the frozen man into the cabin; I awake facing the cabin wall; I see a grey light coming through a crack; drifting snow sifts between heavy wooden shutters; a few dying embers in the fireplace allows me to start a fire; as I pull the man into the bunk bed, there is a noise with the clattering racket of roof shingles in concert with a hum of streaming wind over the ledge; the storm stops; blinding sunlight sets the snow drifts ablaze, sparkling over the entire mountainside; huge quantities of snow has buried the cabin et a few yards away is a barren spot etched by the raging summit winds; I open a door beside the fireplace; a frozen deer carcass hangs by some pots and a hatchet; I realize I can boil some meat; I hear the man moaning; I rush back into the room; I take off his jacket; I scream; it is Duncan's face!

[2 weeks later]

Dr. Johns meets with Christine and has a session with her.

DR. JOHNS (Upon leaving)

Goodbye Christine.

JOSEPHINE (Startled)

That's Miss Margo Curry, Doctor Johns!

DR. JOHNS

Oh, I meant Margo. I apologize. Thank you for coming Margo.

29. INT/DR JOHNS' OFFICE—DAY

DR. JOHNS

I notice you have had a new haircut.

CHRISTINE

Yes, I didn't think you doctors noticed that sort of thing.

DR. JOHNS

You didn't notice I was a man? I notice your lips and check bones and lovely eyes, and I could go on and on which would be quite unprofessional of me. But what the heck. You are a beautiful human being. Your Father was right when he told his wife that you were basically good looking even then.

CHRISTINE

Well I'm starting to see you in a different light.

DR. JOHNS

Speaking of light I've never examined your eyes or even given you a neurological examination.

Even though, your family physician, said your neurological aspects are normal. I need to see for myself. Do you mind?

CHRISTINE

No of course not.

DR. JOHNS

I'll just check your elbow, patellar, ankle and wrist reflexes. O.K. there now. Next let me look into your eyes, with this ophthalmoscope. We'll need to turn off the room light. Duncan's lips are within an inch of Christine's. He quickly turns on the light in the room.

CHRISTINE

How were my eyes?

DR.JOHNS

Sensa....oh, ah, no signs of glaucoma, macular degeneration, flame hemorrhages, retinitis or cataracts.

[Christine smiles.]

DR. JOHNS (facetiously)

At least we know that you don't have a malignant gliobastoma that is causing you to have nightmares.

CHRISTINE (to herself)

He is quite a handsome doctor.

30. INT/MR. CURRY'S HOUSE—NIGHT

CHRISTINE

I never really remember you and Mother showing love or affection for each other. I only remember her as an advisory to you. I never understood why you stayed with her for so long after she began drinking so much.

MR. CURRY

Let me explain it this way. Everything was fine the first years we were married. She started to get lonely, not that I didn't give her attention. She seemed to just slip from one occasional beer or two to more and more. From there on it simply developed into a sad state that eventually caused me to leave my two great children. I'm so sorry. Please don't hate me.

MR. CURRY

Good night Christine. By the way, you don't seem to be having as many nightmares lately.

CHRISTINE

I'm not having any nightmares.

MR. CURRY

Dr. Johns must be doing a good job on you.

CHRISTINE

Dr. Johns is doing a wonderful job on me.

[A little later-dream state for Christine, sepia colored, somewhat blurry]

I seem to be in a small boat in a large lake and it has huge wave. I think I'm going to drown. Help! Help! A man is rowing towards me. We are on shore going into a cabin out of a torrential rain.

31. INT/CABIN—NIGHT

The man throws wood on the fireplace.

MAN

Take off your clothes.

CHRISTINE

What?

MAN

Don't get prudish on me. You may die of shock, Get those things off. Then I'll dry you off with this probably clean towel.

CHRISTINE (as she undresses)

Probably?

MAN (drying her hair)

Turn away from the fire if it is too hot for you-just step away form it a bit.

CHRISTINE (shivering)

If this were some other circumstance, I think I would find this quite erotic.

MAN

Here's some underwear. Climb into that bed. Do you feel better now?

CHRISTINE

Yes, But where are you sleeping?

MAN

With you—never mind, I'm just a harmless goat.

32. EXT/DOORWAY OF CABIN—DAY

MAN

Good morning. I thought since there was a woman around, I'd shave.

CHRISTINE

It's you Duncan!

33. INT/DR.JOHNS' OFFICE—DAY

DR. JOHNS

What's new?

CHRISTINE

I've been having dreams.

DR. JOHNS

I asked what's new. Yes, I know you have dreams but hopefully not as many.

CHRISTINE

These are not those types of dreams.

DR. JOHNS

Oh.

CHRISTINE

Let me put it this way. In the last two dreams you have saved my life.

DR. JOHNS

That's good.

CHRISTINE

But in the second one not only did you save my life but it was the most erotic dream I have ever had. You were toweling me down and I was completely nude.

DR. JOHNS

Whoa! This may lead to more than I need to know.

CHRISTINE (upon leaving)

You're the psychiatrist.

FO

FI

34.INT/DR. JOHNS'OFFICE—DAY

DR. JOHNS (to himself)

(That beige suite, orange lipstick and new coiffure makes Christine a very good looking gal. Who would have known?)

Your looking lovely today Christine. How have you been .Those nightmares should be less frequent? They will eventually disappear now that you have them accounted for and I brought them into your conscious mind so you can grabble with them.

CHRISTINE

I don't have nightmares anymore. I owe you my life—at least my mind.

DR. JOHNS

I'll take you to dinner some evening and we will celebrate. I'll declare you cured. So, our dinner date will be ethical.

CHRISTINE

I'm afraid I would have accepted your invitation no matter what the patient-doctor status was. You see I like you very much.

DR. JOHNS

Thank you for that Christine. I'm also finding you a wonderful person.

DR. JOHNS

Let me take you out. We'll call it a date.

CHRISTINE

Is this correct?

DR. JOHNS

This is another approach I use for all my good looking patients.

CHRISTINE

Well, since you put it that way. Is this going to be all about my case and its progress?

DR. JOHNS

No. It's going to be all about me, me, me. You look surprised.

CHRISTINE

I am. Believe me doctor.

DR. JOHNS

Just call me Duncan.

CHRISTINE (flirtingly)

I still am surprised, Duncan.

35. INT/RESTAURANT—DAY

DUNCAN

We'll start with duck soup and pink champagne. What about grilled prawns later?

CHRISTINE

Sounds delicious. In fact it sounds fabulous. I must get more mental problems if this is the way you treat your patients.

DUNCAN

I'm afraid this is not routine. I got to know you. Now you will get to know me.

CHRISTINE

Before you start, do you have any brothers or sisters?

DUNCAN

No, I'm an only child. I'm from Des Moines, Iowa. My paternal Grandfather raised pigs and my father and I leased a hundred acres of land and grew corn as any proper Iowan should do. My father died of lung cancer from chain smoking.

CHRISTINE

Do you smoke?

DUNCAN

The only time I smoked was when I played pinochle with my Dad and Mother and my wife. We would smoke Mississippi Crooks.

They were actually crooked and kind of wavy and they were rum soaked. My mother died when I was only twenty-three. They never figured out the cause. She died in her sleep. My wife did not die of any exotic disease. She was simply run over at an intersection. We had been very happy on a small farm south of Des Moines while I taught at the university in town.

CHRISTINE

Where did you study psychiatry?

DUNCAN

At the University of Kansas because they were associated with the Menninger Clinic, a very famous psychiatric clinic that I had wanted to attend.

CHRISTINE

Why did you select psychiatry?

DUNCAN

You know I really don't know the answer to that. It just seemed to be less understood as, say, cardiology. It seemed more challenging and just simply more interesting to me I guess.

CHRISTINE

I'm glad you chose psychiatry.

They gaze into each other's eyes.

F.O.

FI

36.INT/DR. JOHNS' OFFICE—DAY

JOSEPHINE

Dr. Johns. Miss Margo Curry says it is urgent that she speak with you.

DR. JOHNS

Come on in Margo. It's good to see you again. What seems to be the problem?

MARGO

I've had a nervous breakdown. Since I've seen you before, I thought I could seek help from you.

DR. JOHNS

Indeed you may. But what makes you think you've had a nervous breakdown?

MARGO

It all started last week when I decided I would visit my father. When he greeted me at the door, instead of him giving me a hug, he stood back as if amazed at seeing me and said hello Christine. I corrected him and said I'm Margo. Well he's old and I thought he just didn't recognize me. He continued to address me as Christine and I became infuriated with him. He always did like Christine better than me and I became enraged. I just snapped, I guess. He seemed quite surprised to see me in such a state, maybe I scared him. Things settled down and I just went along with his calling me Christine. But the next day when I went to the grocery store things got worse. The cashier asked me if I were Christine and I said yes quite easily as if I were her. In fact I met someone who apparently knew Christine and, as I was walking back to the house, he said hello Christine. How are you? And I had no sense of correcting him. I just accepted his remark and said I'm doing fine, thank you and again even felt like I was Christine. Something must have happened to me during the outrage incident with father. I guess since he thought I was Christine it didn't occur to him. I didn't want to be too nosy but I thought it was curious that she wasn't around. Father continued to call me Christine while I was there. He may be getting Alzheimer's.

DR. JOHNS

I don't think you had a nervous breakdown Margo but I do think we need to explore this at another time. So make an appointment as soon as possible with my secretary. Thank you for coming and don't worry about this too much. Good bye Christine.

[Scene]

Dr. Johns realizes his error upon hearing Josephine's goodbye to Margo, Christine simply turns and similes at Duncan. Duncan at that moment knows that Christine knows she is Margo.

DUNCAN

Christine before you pass through that door, permit me ask you a question. Would you allow me to see you at your house at seven o'clock?

CHRISTINE

Yes.

37. EXT/MR. CURRY'HOUSE—NIGHT

Duncan rings the bell. Christine answers the door.

DUNCAN

I wish to tell your something important. You're not Christine! You're not Margo! I'm in love with you Gloria!

He kisses her passionately.

Gloria looks searchingly into Duncan's eyes.

GLORIA

And I'm in love with you. What are your names?

THE END

III

THE PEPPER GRINDER

Registration # 1413280

Introduction

The Pepper Grinder is a stage play and the writer has produced and directed it at the CommRow in Reno in July 2012.

Setting: Upper middle class residential area of suburbia Kansas City, Kansas in the autumn of 1948. Mr. Robert Hendricks's house is next to the Anderson home.

Cast

Beverly (Bev) Sue Anderson (Daughter)
Kathryn Anderson (Bev's Mother)
Jack Anderson (Bev's Father)
Robert Hendricks (Neighbor)
Bea (Bev's Aunt)
JoAnne (Bev's Girlfriend)
Eric (Bev's Ex-boyfriend)
Nurse
Policeman

Furniture

One Bed (Bev's, Hospital's, Robert's, Parent's)
Two Tables (Robert's Kitchen, Anderson's Kitchen, Nurses Desk, Anderson's Dining Table)

One Bench (Robert's Deck, Hospital Waiting Room)
Five Chairs (Anderson's Dining Table)

<u>Miscellaneous:</u>

5 plates, cane, blue table cloth, red checkered table cloth, 5 settings of utensils, 5 glasses, pill box, nurse's uniform, hospital gown, large pepper grinder, salt shaker, chocolate cake, paper plates, binoculars, lemonade (water), two ham sandwiches, gauze, Vaseline strips, tape, mayonnaise jar, lid, phone, magazines, bench (for hospital waiting area), blanket, bandage, and cane.

<u>Acts</u>

Act I

Scene1. Bev's Bedroom (pink-p)
Scene2. Lawn (green-g)/Robert's Kitchen (yellow-y)/Robert's Deck (brown-br/lawn (green-g)/
    Kissing scene (blue-bl)
Scene3. Anderson's Kitchen (yellow-y)/Lawn (green-g)
Scene4. Anderson's Living Room (blue-bl)
Scene5. Hospital (Robert's Room/Waiting Room (white-w)
Scene6. [Same] (white-w)
Scene7. Robert's Front Door/Robert's bedroom (red-r)
Scene8. Anderson's Living Room (blue-bl)
Scene9. Anderson's Living Room (blue-bl)/Robert's Bed Room (red-r)
Scene10. Anderson's Living Room (blue-bl)
Scene11. Spy Segment and Central Park (green-g)/ Highway (white-w)
Scene12. Anderson's Living Room (blue-bl)

Act II

Scene1. Anderson's Living Room [Party] (blue-bl) / Lawn (green-g)
Scene2. Anderson's Dining Room (orange-o)
Scene3. [Same/ Dénouement] (orange-o)

Act I

[Curtain]

Scene 1. (p)

[Bev JoAnne, and Eric are in Bev's bedroom on the bed looking through movie magazines. Eric is on the bed, JoAnne is across the room on a chair.] JoAnne: "I think Betty Gable is beautiful"

[JoAnne stands up crosses over to Bev handing her the magazine. Bev takes the magazine and falls back onto the bed on to her back twisting the magazine as she peruses the photo]

Bev: "Her legs are shapely but her cheeks remind me of a chipmunk stuffed with nuts because she still has baby fat in her face"

[A light knock on the door as it opens.]

Kathryn: "Didn't you hear me about twenty minutes ago asking you to help with the dishes? I swear you are the most irresponsible person in the world. JoAnne If your mother told you to go to the kitchen and help her would you still be lying on the bed? No need to answer. Why should you have to compare yourself with others? Your father and I are seriously considering you, Beverly Sue, at the age of eighteen of your enlisting in the army. It will be the only way to save your soul and our sanity.

Bev: (Sarcastically) "Thank you Mother for the support you've shown me during my difficult teen years."

[Kathryn stomps out of the doorway. Bev throws the magazine she is holding at the door].

JoAnne: "Why are you so mad at your mother all the time?"

Bev: Why? Well it's pretty plain why. She's a wreck, a complete wreck. Why did I have to end up with worst Mother in the neighborhood? How is that? How does that work out anyway? I should have had some say in the matter since I have to live with her."

[Kathryn returns into the light and once again and appears at Bev's door.]

Kathryn: "JoAnne I want you to leave and not return until your mother says it is alright. I will be in touch with her. Also I want your boyfriend to go home this very minute."

[Eric and JoAnne leave]

Bev: "You can't do this. You can't tell me what my friends can do and can't do."

Kathryn: (stepping through the door) "You wanta bet? Sometimes I wish you were never born."

Bev: "That was a low blow!"

Kathryn: "Sorry. I didn't mean that."

Bev: "Get out! Get out! I hate you. I hate you. I hate you. Bitch. [(Pause) Katherine leaves the spot.] "Is this all there is to life? It's horrible, horrible."

[Curtain]

Scene 2.

[Bev goes from bedroom and enters out onto the lawn (stage left-g), meandering at first to the left (stage left) and then turning back to the right (stage right] towards her neighbor's. Wiping her eyes she notices her new neighbor.]

Robert: "Hi."

Bev: "Hi."

Robert: "I'm your new neighbor, just moved in a couple of weeks ago."

Bev: "Yeah. I know. I've seen you out on your deck. What's your name?" [Making a quick swipe with her arm to her eyes to make sure there were no tears.]

Robert: "Robert. What's yours?"

Bev: "Bev –where did you move from?"

Robert: "My parents live in Connecticut.

Bev: "Did you bring your family with you?"

Robert: "I don't have a wife and kids but I do have my own chemical company."

Bev: "Wow"

Robert: "Say, why don't you come up to the kitchen so we can get better acquainted. I was just going to fix some lunch. Have you had lunch yet? Why don't you come in and we'll make some ham sandwiches."

Bev: "Oh. Thanks, but I'm not allowed…..O.K. Good idea."

[Curtain]

(y)[Bev and Robert are standing by the kitchen table.]

Robert: "I'll get the ham if you smear the mayonnaise."

[Bev drops the mayonnaise jar lid on the floor. They both simultaneously bend over to get the lid. Their faces meet and slowly they come to a kiss.]

(Pause)

Bev: "Oh my. I've never felt a kiss like that. It's almost magical."

Robert: "I must agree with you, that kiss was different. [Rising to a standing position Robert says.] Let's try that again."

Bev: [Very quickly and enthusiastically replies] "Yeah –let's."

[They kiss a longer kiss this time embracing each other.]

(Pause)

Bev: "Toto I don't think we're in Kansas anymore."

Robert: "My name isn't Toto and we are in Kansas. I think we are." [A little dazed] "We'd better have our ham sandwiches."

[Fade to black (note: remove folded screen)]

[Both go out on the deck (br), put down their plates and lemonade glasses and proceed to look into each other's faces, not eating, not moving, as if they were a little afraid of each other.]

Robert: "What happened in there?"

Bev: "I don't know. We were just fixing sandwiches. (Pause) Do you think I'm cute?"

Robert:" Sure you're cute.-more than that you are a charmer. I never realized that a girl so young could be charming. I always considered a thirty year old as having that possibility. I've really never known a girl as young as you. How old are you?

Bev: "Ah.. I'm, ah… 16. How old are you?

Robert: "Ah… I'm 27. What do you think about most of the time? I mean what do you like to do?"

Bev: "I don't know. I'm interested in movie stars and I go to all our High School basketball games."

Robert: "I heard you arguing with your Mother from clear out here. Why don't you get along with your Mother? (Pause)

Bev: "She just doesn't understand me."

Robert: "Mothers are important you know, though I really can't say too much because I never really knew my Mother or Dad. You know, really well. We were never close. My Mother was very strict. I was smothered by her upbringing- there being no one else to give rules to. By this same reason I never got to know my Father. How about your Father?"

Bev: "He's alright, I guess, he doesn't bother me much and I don't bother him. I don't think he thinks much of me, but why should he? I'm not much."

Robert: "What in the world to you mean by that Bev? You seem like a wonderful person to me."

Bev: "Tell that to my parents."

[Curtain]

[Both go back onto the lawn (g)]

Kathryn: [Yelling from next door] "Beverly Sue Anderson where are you?"

Bev: "I've got to go."

[Bev walks away from Robert to the right]

Robert: "When will I see you again?"

Bev. "Quicker than quick."

[Bev return to Robert –Kissing scene—Ballet-bl]

[Curtain]

Scene 3.

[The Anderson's kitchen (y) at 7:30 AM. Kathryn in bewilderment disgustedly watches as Bev throws together her lunch in a haphazardly way and dashes out the front door through the living room without saying a word.]

Kathryn: "What in the hell was that? What has gotten into that child?"

[Curtain]

[Bev then (g) crosses over to Robert's house, checking behind her as she approaches his deck door. She starts to knock but arms reach out and grab her into the doorway [out of the light]. A moment later Bev returns to the light and cautiously passes on over the lawn exiting to the middle curtain slit.]

Scene 4.

[The Anderson's Living Room (bl) two days later].

Kathryn: [Speaking to Bev who is writing] "Did you hear about the accident our neighbor Mr. Hendricks [Bev drops pen but is expressionless] had at work two days ago. Mr. Wilson told me he was in intensive care for a day but is out now in a private room but he is still unconscious. Apparently a beaker containing some very toxic chemical broke on the floor cutting his foot."

Bev: "I hadn't heard about it."

Kathryn: "Someone needs to represent us and go visit him- at least make some inquiry at the hospital as to his condition. I understand his parents have to delay their flight here because of some other major family problem. (Pause) Will you go to the hospital? I am so busy with the Ladies Aid meeting today."

Bev: "I don't have time for this sort of thing. I'm trying to get into the auditions for the school play. Besides there will always be someone sick or dying in this neighborhood. When does a person have time to live their own life?"

Kathryn: "That's my daughter, the sympathetic, empathetic Red Cross worker of the world. Never ever thinking of herself. Alright, said the little red hen. I guess I will go but it won't be till 5 o'clock. (Pause) Go, Go then- back upstairs with you. Just get out of my sight."

[Curtain]

Scene 5.

(w) [A small city hospital. The patient's room on left front stage ends by a divider where the nurse's desk and waiting room area contains a bench on the remaining right area. Kathryn walks up to the nurse.]

Kathryn: "I would like to inquire as to Mr. Hendricks' condition."

Nurse: "He remains unconscious. There is someone with him at the moment, if you would care to wait."

Kathryn: "That will be fine."

[The nurse leaves her desk through the mid-curtain slit. Kathryn returns to the seat and then. Kathryn approaches the divider looking back first and then, peaking around the divider and is shocked to see Bev, Bev is hugging Robert's left arm and hand, sobbing profusely. Kathryn bites her arm so as not to speak out and stumbles out of the hospital dazed and confused.]

[Curtain]

Scene 6.

[Bev returns the next day to the hospital.]

Bev: [asks the nurse], "How is … "[but before she can finish the nurse speaks.]

Nurse: "Robert is awake and……"

[Bev dashes into Robert's room.] "..and you may see him.." [The nurse looking bewildered shrugs her shoulders]

[Bev begins frantically kissing Robert all over his face.]

Bev: "Don't you ever, ever do anything like that again. To think you could have left me forever. [She cries loudly. Robert begins fighting her off and yells for the nurse.] "I love you, I love you." [Bev is hysterical.]

Robert: "Take her away before she kills me."

[The nurse drags Bev from the room and sits her down on the bench. She goes to her table and takes a bottle of pills to Bev.]

Nurse: "Here take this Miss Anderson. It will calm you down, we are trying to save lives here-not end them. Now we do need someone to manage his foot bandages in an aseptic manner. I understand that you live near the patient's place. Could you come tomorrow at 2:30 and we will demonstrate how this is done?"

Bev: "2:30? Oh no. I couldn't possibly…I'll be here."

Nurse: "We are going to dismiss him the day after tomorrow."

Bev: "I apologize for acting the way I did. You see I love him very much."

Nurse: [Sarcastically] "You're kidding."

Bev: "Thanks for the sedative. Goodbye. Oh yeah. See you tomorrow."

[Curtain]

Scene 7.

[Kathryn has arrived in the car with Robert having gone to get him from the hospital. Bev has agreed only to meet them to help Kathryn get Robert with his right foot bandaged up to his bedroom. (r)]

Kathryn: [Helping Robert out of the back seat of the car into the light (r)] "Here we are. Let us help you out of the car. I'll have to apologize for Bev's not coming to the hospital but she has been gracious enough [sarcastically] to assist us now."

Robert: "Oh, everything will be fine."

Bev: "Wait a minute. Let me get Mr. Hendricks' cane."

[Bev steps out of the light for a moment and returns into the light with a cane]

Kathryn: "How did you know he had a cane?"

Bev: "Well ah….. (stumble sentence)… most people with an injured foot would have a cane or crutch or something." (Loud) [Important in Act II]

Kathryn: "Here I'll put your phone on your bedside table so you can call us for any reason."

Robert: "Thank you Mrs. Anderson and Beverly Sue. Did I tell you two that my parents called and I told them that I've practically recovered? Actually, I think I will call them now, so I can convince them not to try and come out to see me."

[Curtain]

Scene 8. (bl) [Anderson living room]

Kathryn: "Beverly, why can't we be friends? I'm sorry. I really didn't mean those things I said out of anger, but you are so easy to incite anger."

Bev: "Well if you would just leave me and my friends alone and stop interfering with my life. I need some space, some room. My likes will not always be your likes."

Kathryn: "I'll try. I must admit I do not approve of a lot of your friends, especially the boys you've managed to hang out with recently. They're going to lead you into trouble-mind my word which I'm sure you won't. Maybe I should make Jack take on more responsibility of raising you."

[Fade out]

[Jack is in the living room (bl) with Bev]

Jack: "Come, sit beside me Bev. (Pause) Something I never told you about your Mother. Kathryn use to go to a dance studio when she was about nineteen years old. She loved to dance. Well I didn't give two hoops and a holler for dancing. But we ended up meeting in that dance studio with its little band. Ralph a buddy of mine begged us one evening to accompany him to this studio. All the girls sat on chairs on the side and the guys would simply choose and proceeded to ask the girl if she wished to dance. The rest is history. I think we've gone out dancing maybe three times all these years we've been married. Kind of sad. Huh?"

Bev: "Why don't you ever take mother dancing now?"

Jack: "I don't know. Time just slips by with a million other things. It's the Judeo-Christian work ethic that eats us all up and doesn't even leave the bones. Sometimes I feel sorry for her but then again she is filled with her own life-she's left me out of it to a large extent."

Bev: "Thanks for telling me that Father. I think I understand Mother a little better now. I even feel a little sorry for her too. She hasn't had a nice social life. But I don't understand you. How could you have been the head of a construction crew or whatever you did and not be domineering over Mother. She runs this place and you let her."

Jack: "It's easier that way."

Bev: "What keeps you two together?"

Jack: "You mean divorce?"

Bev: "Exactly."

Jack: "Well, she manages to manage you. I could never have done that feat."

[Bev smiles] Bev: "You be nice."

Jack: "Actually about ten years ago we were near that stage but we managed to talk ourselves out of it."

Bev: "My gosh! The stuff I don't know about my own parents. How can I help you and Mother be happier together? I'm just bubbling over with happiness. I've got happiness to spare. Let me do something for you."

Jack: "Why are you so happy?"

Bev: (Coyly) "You might be surprised"

Jack: "You probably need to work on your Mother first. She's your patient most in need. You know I have a feeling you could straighten her out given time. I suggest you be subtle about this. You and I will conspire to remake Kathryn, the unmovable. Yeah, I like that idea."

[Kathryn enters from stage left]

Jack: "Listen Bev, your mother and I are going out to the weekend cabin for a few days. We'll leave this evening."

Kathryn (to Bev): "Now remember-no parties and get your homework done."

[Bev goes to her room without comment. Kathryn checks to make sure Bev is in her room and out of hearing distance.]

Kathryn: "I don't know what's been going on between those two, but I'm going to nail him. You just wait and see. The very idea of that man with our under-aged daughter right under our noses".

Jack: "What are you going to do? Drive back from the cabin this evening?"

Kathryn: "What if I hide in his house? He can't get around."

Jack: "Where would you hide? –in the kitchen-Bev will be there,-in the bedroom-Robert will be there,-in the bathroom,-there's not room for all of you to be there, -in the living room,- they are never there. It's ridiculous. Kathryn, get a hold of yourself."

Kathryn: "No. I'm not going. I'm going to stay and you leave without me. I'll 'camp out' in our bedroom very discreetly. We'll just see what 'hanky-panky' is going on around here. Bev should feel free to do whatever she's been doing. Be sure and leave these binoculars with me before you go. I'll use the other car and may come up and join you at the cabin later tomorrow. If not, you come back here when Bev's at school. One way or the other I'll report to you all of the night time activities around this place. If she finds me here, I'll simply say that I felt ill and decided not to go with you to the cabin."

Jack: "Are you sure you know what you're doing?"

Kathryn:" No. But I'm going to do it anyway."

[Jack exists stage left while shaking his head in bewilderment. When Kathryn hears Bev leave her room, she looks up to the ceiling to hear and then carefully 'tippy toes' to the living room window facing the lawn to the folded screen where she watches Bev through the window with her binoculars.]

Kathryn: "There's that innocent daughter of mine running over to that no good neighbor."

[Curtain-change props]

Scene 9

[Bev enters from stage right to Robert's bedroom (r)]

Bev: "Hi. How's you doin? I'm going to change the bandages. Have no fear nurse Higginsbottom is here." [They both laugh. Bev deftly begins to change the dressings. Kathryn remains at the edge of the blue flood and is using binoculars]

Kathryn: [In amazement-speaks out loud to herself] "I don't believe it. She's acting like a registered nurse. How does she know how to do those things? Don't I know anything at all about my daughter? Ah…she has shut the blinds. [Kathryn exits the blue flood]

Bev: "I'm really doing well at school right now. I wonder what Mother thinks about that. I wonder what I think about that. What in the world is making the change? The only thing is that I notice I always have you to worry about and take care of, yet I have more time for home work. That does <u>not</u> make sense. I haven't seen a movie magazine in ages. Was I spending that much time reading those things? And poor JoAnne probably thinks I don't like her anymore."

Robert: "I love you so much; I can hardly stand to be awake knowing I will next be asleep and not loving you for those moments. I want to know everything about you."

Bev:" I don't think so."

Robert: "You say you love me and I believe you with all my heart. I don't really know how to tell you this, but it's something I've been thinking about. A couple falls in love and the intensity of love and sex over the following years wanes and waxes. But I figured out one aspect that fades so quickly-it is forgotten so abruptly. You know what that is?"

Bev: "I'm sorry I'm just a teen ager-remember? We're not allowed to think about anything but puppy love and sex."

Robert: "I made a little rhyme about what I'm about to tell you. Love and sex waxes and wanes, but affection should always remain. Well, the way I see it, people are missing ninety percent of what a couple should be doing. It's giving affection to each other. Think about this. Affection cannot be asked for. I can't ask you to be affectionate towards me or give me affection. Then it's just something on demand. It's no longer affection. It's just a nibble on my ear. Whereas, if you nibbled on my ear spontaneously, I would turn and kiss you on your nose. We were both being affectionate to each other. Get it?"

Bev: "Yes I do. That's really good thinking and I promise never to ask you to be affectionate, but I also promise to be a loving and affectionate wife."

Robert: "You know I dreamed last night about you. We were on a train to somewhere and you had broken your leg. I carried you to the observation car and we watched the stars together."

Bev: "Robert you just want to have some excuse to take care of me. That's all that dream meant."

Robert: "Pretty clever young rascal. You have been reading Freud. But I think you may be right."

Bev: "Enough of this heavy conversation. Let's go out on the lawn."

[Curtain]

[Lawn-(g)]

(g) Bev: "Now don't you think this was a good idea getting you out into the fresh evening air? Let me spread the blanket out on the back lawn here."

[Bev speaks after she carefully helps him onto the blanket.]"

Bev: "What are you thinking about?" [Bev began searching each hair on the back of Robert's neck like a monkey searching for lice."

Robert: "Stop that, it tickles."

Bev: (teasingly) "And why should I care?"

Robert: "I found out about your boyfriend Eric. I'll come right out and say it. I'm terribly jealous. Let me put it in philosophical terms. You know most people don't even exist. They never will exist. But a few do exist. Most of them are dead. But still a fraction of those that exist are alive at this moment- their whole life being only a moment of eternity. So this is that moment that we can touch and love each other. Don't spend another wasted moment with that so called boyfriend of yours."

Bev:" (Surprised) I didn't intend to-I won't –I promise. Now I'll give <u>you</u> some philosophy. Did you know that you and I are the only ones that exist? I feel that way sometimes. That all the rest simply get in our way. I like some of them and I dislike others but they all actually just get in our way. I just want there to be you and me and the stars."

Robert: "Let me read you a poem I wrote. Oh, I've got it right her" [he reaches into his pocket].

> "Where for do I come from?
> Who am I? What is "I"?
> Why not a dog am I, or a lovely butterfly?
> Just why am I, I?

This business of being, being an I.
This individual that is recognized as I.
Who is this person, this mind called I?
I a product of genetics and environ.
I could have been you, someone else.
Or maybe I am, I know not for sure.
But where are the other I's?
The I's that could have been.
The I's done past and future to be.
The I's already dead.
I am changing by the second.
I am changing you, you are changing me.
I am still called I.
But the previous I is gone.
Where am I, or-
Am I?
Do you like it?"

Bev: "It's marvelous. Who would know you were a biochemist.

Robert: "I'm going to write a poem just for you. I have lots of time lying around with this foot."

Bev: "They say you become extremely aware of surfaces and textures if you are really in love.

I just realized that explains when I touch you it is different than when I touch Eric. I thought I was just a little crazy." [Bev tickles Robert under his arm and he jumps] "I'm surprise to find you so ticklish. Somehow I imagined you to be a man of steel and not have some feature of a kid."

Robert: "Lots of adults are ticklish. Now let's see about you. [Robert tries to chase Bev; hobbling around the grassy area and Bev screams with glee.] I wonder if we're doing the right thing by letting this go on."

Bev: (With great anxiety) "Oh Robert don't toss me away. This is not some puppy love. You know it isn't. This is got to be a real thing. We must protect our feelings, not just get rid of them like they were last week fling. [She starts to weep.]"

Robert: "Here let me wipe some of those tears. There should never be any tears from your eyes but I'm afraid you'll always have a few nearby because you're so loving and kind. Oh how I love

151

you. You're right. It must be right. If this is wrong, then the rest of the world is wrong. Why should your lips be softer than mine? Why should your hair be softer than mine? Why should your skin be softer than mine? Why should your gaze be softer than mine?"

Bev: "You know I'm realizing a lot about my family, because of the feelings I have for you. For instance, I know now what my family is all about. They are in search of affection. My Mother is what she is today because she couldn't find affection from my Father. So she hides from affection now making herself stern and basically unloving. I'm starting to realize why people are the way they are. Ha-ha and you thought I couldn't think maturely."

Robert: "You're sure getting there fast-don't think too maturely. I may love you for just the way you are-a young punk."

Bev: "I may just let you get up to the bedroom by yourself smarty pants."

Robert: "You don't realize how interesting it has been these past weeks just being around you. Your young mind is so wonderful. It's like a playpen with a child. The only confinement is the imagination of the child within and that is endless." [As they exit stage right]

[Curtain]

Scene 10

[Jack enters from stage left and sits in couch. Kathryn enters from stage left a moment later and sits on chair in the Anderson living room (bl).]

Kathryn: "I could hear her, Jack, rattling her books and papers."

Jack: "Her grades have improved remarkably."

Kathryn: "What is going on with that child? Jack- you go back to the cabin. I'll drive up later. I'm going to figure this out if, If…oh, I don't know. What do I know? I don't seem to know anything anymore."

[Kathryn begins sobbing]

Jack: "I can't stand to see you cry Kathryn. What's the matter?"

Kathryn: "It just seems that I don't know my own child. I can't stand that." [She continues crying.]

Jack: "Of course you don't know her. She's growing up and becoming a different person."

Kathryn: "Jack do you think I'm mean-spirited?"

Jack: "No not at all. You're just a 'son of a, I mean, girl of a bitch." Just kidding (Pause) you're motivated to make sure your daughter gets off to the right start. Not that she has been getting off to the right start lately. Let's face it whatever you have done to this point hasn't changed a thing."

Kathryn: "Maybe I should let what happens happen. But I just can't. I can't stand by and then regret what ever does happen."

Jack: "What <u>has</u> happened?"

Kathryn: "Nothing has happened."

Jack: "Well there you are."

[They leave stage left]

[Fade]

[The living room (bl) is empty when Bev first steps in then followed by Aunt Bea from stage left. Both are sitting together on couch.]

Bev: "I like to ask you a very personal question Aunt Bea. Have you ever been in love?"

Aunt Bea: "Of course, just because I never married is no reason I haven't had my day. As it turned out, my moving elsewhere and parental pressures were major elements in interfering with the fact that no marriages ever developed. All the time now I managed to just barely live with myself with these memories."

Bev: "How sad. I think I shall not let that happen to me. Why don't you get romantic and go on the prowl?"

Aunt Bea: "Simply because I'm too old and fat. I never quite understood why old and overweight go hand in hand or should I say rear in rear. I've heard that even old mice are fat."

[Curtain]

[Flood-g]

Scene 11.

Kathryn: [Mumbling to herself looking through binoculars] "At last some activity. Into the Roberts house goes JoAnne, in goes Bev, now there're helping Robert out to the street and into his car. Back in goes Bev. She has a picnic basket and a blanket. So this may be the moment –the 'coup de gras.' I'll just follow them in my car. How exciting-just like a private eye in a movie. [Fade] I can tell now that they are going to the Central Park. I'll park over here where I can see them nicely."

[This segment is to be acted out silently by Robert, Bev and JoAnne-without dialogue]

[Kathryn stands at edge of orange flood light]

Kathryn: "They have put the blanket down. They are having a picnic. Well what did you expect Kathryn? [JoAnne moves to stage back right as if climbing onto the top of a big boulder.] She has climbed upon a big bolder apparently as a look out. Ah, so Bev and Robert can be secluded under the blanket. But they are remaining exposed on top, just sunbathing and holding hands. JoAnne is shouting to them. They are quickly packing. Then leave. I guess some of Bev's school chums were coming their way and they want this relationship to be kept secret-so much for that escapade."

[Fade with slight orange; Keep lighting dim.]

[Kathryn moves to highway spy area with her binoculars; dimly lit vacant stage]

Kathryn: "It's getting late and dark. I'll get out of the car so I can observe Robert's house. But I see Bev going over to Robert's house stopping in the kitchen, up to his bedroom and serving his meal to him in bed, she's holding one of his hands while he's eating-really now [disgustedly,] -tucks him in, returning to our house, goes up to her bedroom and begins studying. How utterly boring. Oh! Hello officer. What are you doing out this late?"

Police Officer: "Well now, if it isn't Mrs. Anderson. What are <u>you</u> doing out this late-binoculars in hand?"

Kathryn: "Ah... would you believe bird watching? Umm. (Pause) My car stopped. Must be vapor locked or something. I was just seeing if I could tell if my husband was home so I could go fetch him to start my car for me." [Looking quite self-satisfied with her quickly prefabricated explanation.]

Police Officer: "Vapor lock in the cool of the evening-I hardly think so, but let me take a look at it anyway. [He exits spotlight for a moment, returns] There now, It started right up. Next time if anything like this happens, you leave your parking lights on, especially on a curve like this. O.K.?"

Kathryn: "Thank you, officer (Pause)-Whew."

[Curtain]

Scene 12.

[Kathryn and Aunt Bea are in the Anderson living room. (bl)]

Kathryn: (Hysterically) "I can't find Bev anywhere. She's not in her room. I'm going over to Mr. Hendricks' to see if she is over there."

Aunt Bea: "That won't be necessary Kathryn. Many times I've seen her out on her balcony. I should have told you before now, because when I first saw her standing out there on the balcony, I thought she might be attempting to jump-probably over some teen romance. But as the nights went on she never did anything suspicious, so I just let it go."

Kathryn: "I can hear her on her balcony now and I bet I know what she's looking at. Let's just check in on Robert's deck. [Kathryn goes over to marked area on screen that denotes a window]. There he is. Exactly. They are looking at each other in the moonlight. I give up."

[Aunt Bea exits stage left]

[Jack walks into the living room from stage left.]

Jack: "Well have you pinned the goods on Robert that will put him away for a decade as a sex fiend? I, myself, don't really give a good G.D. Let her have some kicks. I'm sure you did."

Kathryn:" Really Jack, I never even knew you knew the word "kicks".

Jack: "Look I have a thought. I don't really know how it might work out but my idea would be to put Bev's school buddies including Eric, the guy she is or was so mad about, and Robert in one room-this room."

Kathryn: "Under what pretext?"

Jack: "Just a party. All you need is cake to have a party. I don't know what will happen but something might get resolved."

Kathryn: "Beautiful. I'll start inviting right away and I don't want to forget JoAnne. I owe her an apology. I'll tell Bev that I intend to invite Robert too because he must be lonely."

[Intermission]

Act II

[Curtain]

Scene1.

[The party is on in the Anderson living room. (bl) (Eric is standing in the lower right corner of the room. JoAnne comes into the room stage right and meanders around. The cake and plates are on the center table]

Kathryn: (to JoAnne) "I'm happy to see you could come to our party as it gives me a chance to apologize for that morning. (Pause) I wonder if you could do me a favor, well really a little undercover work and tell me where in the heck Bev goes after school."

Jack: "Well I can tell you that right now. She comes home here and studies."

Kathryn: "I can hardly believe that."

JoAnne: "It's true. It must be because Bev is the sharpest student, in all the classes, at least the ones she takes with me. All though one time and only one time mind you, she was completely caught off guard just gazing out of the window in Mrs. Tull's class and Mrs. Tull had a terrible time finally getting her attention."

[Robert hobbles in with his cane from stage right.]

Kathryn: "Hi. Glad you could make it. Why don't you have a seat right here?"

Robert: "Thanks".

Jack: "How's that foot doing?"

Robert: "Much better, thanks."

[Bev enters the room from stage right.]

Bev: "Hello Mr. Hendricks. May I get you some cake?"

Robert: "Please"

Eric: [Speaking to Bev but gesturing towards Robert] "How is the old crippled man?"

[Bev takes a piece of cake onto a plate but her hands begin tightening around the piece of cake she is to take to Robert and starts staring at Eric, stares that could kill. She continues to crush the cake in her hand as she tightens her fists but does not budge from her position. Eric quickly moves stumbles back away from Bev towards Aunt Bea.]

Aunt Bea: "What's the story Eric?"

Eric: "I don't know. I don't even remember what I said. Something about the old goat with the cane. I wonder."

Aunt Bea: "I think you've just released your girlfriend to an old goat."

Eric: "I think you may be right. This party is a bust. I need some laughs. I'm going to split this cake thing."

Kathryn: "Beverly Sue you might want to get another more appropriate piece of cake for Robert." Bev recovers out of her trance and realizes the mess in her hand and rushes over to the table wiping her hands.]

Bev: (handing the piece of cake to Robert and dangerously whispers "How I adore you."

Kathryn: [to Bev] "Why don't you ask Robert if he would like for you to go on a movie date? He must be quite lonely."

Bev: [Surprised] "Really Mother. He probably has many sophisticated women he would rather date than a teenage 'bobby-socker'."

Kathryn: "Well, do me a favor and ask him anyway and help him back to his house please."

[Curtain-(g)]

(g)[Bev and Robert are walking towards Robert's deck mumbling to each other.]

Robert: "You look just like a girl I would like to pick up."

Bev: (flirtatiously) "Why Mr. Hendricks"

Robert: "You know I often in my day dreams think of snuggling up to you by a fireplace."

Bev: "And?"

Robert: "None of your business-you're just a teenager –too young for those thoughts."

Bev: "You want me to pin you? I was one of the better wrestlers on the girl's high school team.

Can you believe it? Mother wants me to ask you if you'd like to go to the movies with me and she used the word 'date'"

Robert: "How could I not fall in love with you whenever I see those lovely honey-brown eyes that hold so much love for me-thank you. Incidentally, aren't you supposed to be helping me back?"

Bev: "If I get any closer I'll grab you viciously-never to let you go."

Robert: "Your party was hardly a party."

Bev: "I don't know if it was Father or Mother that had this brilliant idea. But I don't care. It was a chance to be with you once more."

Robert: "I've got an idea. Ask your mother if she would fix dinner for me, not that I don't like your cooking, darling."

[Bev punches him on the arm and then realizes she might have been seen, so quickly glances back.]

Bev: "Good idea. I'll have mother call you regarding the details By the way, I've been meaning to ask you –why do you love me?"

Robert: "Because you are you and not someone else. [Robert kisses Bev's closed eyes] "Wait a minute. I've written you my poem. Let me step inside the doorway [edge of the lawn (g)]for just a minute. Let me see. It should be right here with these papers. Yes. Here it is."

[Robert returns from inside the doorway to the lawn (g-flood) and begins to read.]

> The incredible excitement
> I have known with you.
> Tears stream down my cheeks
> Not the same, never would be the same
> We who had held hands
> on a dark night
> We who had laughed
> ridiculous laughs
> We who had loved
> the warmth of each other
> and shared the emotions
> of a Fall night
> I will search for your smile
> The c harm from just one person
> Incredible
> I search into other's faces
> to find that same smile
> Meaningless
> Yet I search
> Fooling myself into thinking
> that some other's
> would substitute
> That endearing look of kindness
> That once in the world of time
> Could there possibly be
> in front of me-the same
> How frail time is
> How fleeting the precious moments

The tears continue to stream
How long can they stream?
How much of you is me?
How much of me is now you?
Can time destroy?
Nothing
Not distance, not time
Having seen those honey- brown eyes
Nothing can destroy the images of you
I now understand universality
The passion that extends
beyond passion
The soul of you
The beauty of you
The goodness of you
You are heaven
You are earth
I will pass through days
That grow into a continuum
of words
Words only vaguely
to be heard and recognized
I limp in the dark streets
Three walk by
What are they thinking?
What are they saying?
I would not have understood
For I am a million light years away
And they are in the world of reality
At last
Something to bring me back
Back to this world-
a beautiful image of you.

Robert: "You had better return to the party." [Robert's fingers moved gently across Bev's lower lip.]

Bev: "I can't believe I moved you to write that beautiful poem. You must love me very much."

[Curtain]

Scene 2.

[The Anderson's dining room (o).]

Jack: "So what is it you do?"

Robert: "I run a small chemical company. I discovered a process by which we can make the major part of the steroid hormone cheaply. Then other large pharmaceutical companies buy our basic product and do things to it for their own end products-say some drug. What is your business?"

Jack: "I was in construction contracting, but I've been retired for three years now."

Kathryn: "Bev's still upstairs. Bev come on down. We're about to have dinner and your guests have been here for some time."

[All are seated as Bev slinks onto the stage slowly. She shocks everyone. Actors mumbled among themselves. She is wearing a low cut black dress with a black choker around her neck and high heels. Her makeup is immaculate. She looks like a twenty year old model. They all stand in awe.]

(Pause)

Aunt Bea: "Simply stunning. I would never have known it was you."

Jack: "I can't believe this can be my little girl."

Robert: (cautiously) "Are you sure you're not Bev's older sister?"

Kathryn: (Sincerely) "You're a beautiful lady."

Bev: "Oh, this old rag. I had it secretly stored away in my closet for prom night, but I thought this to be a nice occasion for such a dress."

[Everyone sits at the table]

Kathryn: "I don't think the pork roast is quite done. So, why don't you pass around the sliced tomatoes?"

Bev: "Let's see, (Pause) Mr. Hendricks, we've only met twice. Isn't that right? I first saw you when I helped Mother take you up to the bedroom when you came home from the hospital and then again at the cake party."

Robert: "ah…ah…Yes. I guess you're right about that. Umm-interesting. I somehow didn't realize that. I apologize for not asking you over sooner so we can become acquainted."

[Kathryn smirks slightly]

[The tomatoes are dutifully passed about and there is general chatter between Jack and Aunt Bea and Robert and Kathryn.]

Bev: "Here is the salt JoAnne and here Robert is the pepper grinder. I know you ALWAYS have pepper on your tomatoes."

(There is a long silence)

[In the complete silence, Bev drops the pepper grinder on Robert's plate as she is handing it over to him causing a loud noise. She begins to mumble nervously.]

"Some people use pepper on their tomatoes."

[Her lower lip begins to quiver. Tears 'well up' in her eyes as Kathryn stares unemotionally at Bev. Bev begins realizing her 'faux pas' and her breathing increases. Her mind rapidly passes through the thought that her love relationship with Robert may be stopped by her parents. She looks at Kathryn and begins shaking. Bev pushes back, crying out pitifully and in great mental anguish. Bursting into tears -"Ma ma! Ma ma!." She nervously tries to escape –pushes the chair behind her releasing herself and reaches to the ceiling screaming once then twice. Jack and Aunt Bea are flabbergasted. Robert begins to get out of his chair but Kathryn gestures out to indicate to him to remain seated.]

[Kathryn rises and takes two steps towards Bev. Bev remains with her back to Kathryn.]

(Kathryn with great repose states)

Kathryn: "<u>We all know you're in love with Robert</u>."

[Bev starts to scream again but checks it-choking slightly. Her head shakes back and forth in disbelieve at what her mother has said. She slowly turns facing Kathryn and puts her palms upward and shaking her head as if to say 'But how did you know?', but does not speak.]

Kathryn: "You glow like a thousand moons, you're incredible. Jack and I believe the admiration, affection and love between you and Robert may be the most intense the world has ever witnessed. I stand in awe before you. (Pause) If you wish you can go upstairs and straighten up and return to begin a new life."

[Bev starts to go upstairs stage left, but then turns and rushes, embracing her mother (for a long time) and hugs her father (momentarily) and then ascends the stairs.-goes off spot]

Kathryn: (Dismayed) "That may be the last hug I ever receive from my daughter when she learns of what I've been up to."

[Curtain]

Scene 3.

[Same setting. Bev and Robert are holding hands.]

Robert: "You see we thought if you ever found out how we felt about each other you would surely break it up. We couldn't even contemplate such a thing."

Kathryn: "Well Beverly Sue you may never speak to me again and that goes for you too Robert after you've heard <u>my</u> story. I had gone early to the hospital the day that Bev was sobbing and holding you so dearly. I was, of course, shocked beyond belief, when I saw Bev because I didn't even know she knew you. And since you were 27 and she was only 15, I thought I'd catch you two in a compromising situation and I'd have them take you away Robert."

Robert: [Looking at Bev.] "I thought you said you were 16."

Bev: "I lied."

Robert: "By the way I'm 28-I lied"

Jack: "Sounds like a great way to start a lifelong trusting relationship. I hope it will be a long engagement. Anyway I suggest we give the young couple a toast."

[Aunt Bea, Kathryn, Jack and JoAnne stand and raise their water glasses on high.]

Robert: "You see our love is so strong that we don't need anything but to gaze into each other's eyes-a wondrous thing in its self."

Jack: "Bev I think you just remade Kathryn but you sure didn't use too subtle an approach."

Kathryn: "What are you talking about Jack? Never mind. Close your ears Jack. Now that I see Robert in this new light, He is kind of cute."

Bev: "Keep your claws off of him. He's all mine" embracing his arm tightly.

Kathryn: "I didn't want to let you all know that I knew of your feelings because then I couldn't get to you Robert and I was so determined. But nothing ever happened. Bev up and down your stairs, tucking you in, holding hands on the deck, the amount of time I spent with binoculars- I'm practically cross-eyed at a distance, a picnic that turned out to be a picnic."

Bev: "Mother –really. Besides you almost won with "the cane slip" I made and "the squashed cake"- well you did win in the end with "the lots of pepper on it". But you don't ever have to worry about my never hugging you again. Any mother that would go to that much trouble to keep their daughter out of trouble must love their daughter very much."

[Bev goes over and gives a long hug to her mother, then returns to her seat. They are all seated when the lights dim and Bev says.]

Bev: "Anyone for more pepper?"

THE END

IV

A WRITER'S MIND

Registration # 1447415

Introduction

This play originated from a novel "From an Ensenada Window" written by the author. If done with worldwide settings, it would be an expensive film to make.

1. EXT/HOUSE—DAY

> Once upon a time there was a writer who lived with his girlfriend Carlotta.

[scene]

A man is typing in the hot sun on the porch.

VO

CARLOTTA

> I love Konrad but he was a little kooky. I'm sure it was because he spent so much time writing in the sun.

VO

KONRAD (narrates as he types)

And if my voice cannot be heard
Look into my eyes
And if my eyes cannot be seen
Listen to my heart
And if my heart cannot be felt
Wait a moment
For my soul will combine with yours
And my soul has only two loves
The love of God and the love of you

2. INT/HOUSE—DAY

He stops typing.

> I feel sad about the Cuban composer's death that I heard on the
> morning newscast.

He turns off the radio and gazes out of the open window, looking at the whitecaps of the ocean as a warm breeze passed over his face. He closes the shutter.

VO

NARRATOR

The composer's song "The Breeze and I" comes to him.

KONRAD

That song has always reminded me of the waters of the Gulf of California. I am a writer, I am thirty-two years old and—what on God's green earth am I doing here?

Several rays of light filter through the louvered wood shutters onto the dust laden floor.

Carlotta, I ask you, why in the world did I come all the way from
Bergen, Alberta, to stay in this place?

Unconsciously, his attention shifts to a pattern of light on the edge of the wrought iron bed that stands in the middle of the room. Konrad is rather lanky, although at one time he had been heavyset, but since he is tall, he appears a bit gaunt.

CARLOTTA (to herself)

He is a 'hairy beast' with that curly black chest hair and movement
of his Adam's apple fascinates me. Now he is mumbling.

He begins to type on the veranda.

KONRAD

Carlotta, remember I said if for any reason I was unable to write
here, we would immediately go elsewhere.

Again he walks over to the window and opens the green-stained shutters. The heat from the terra-cotta tile roof below quickly enters into the small room, which has remained chilled by the night air.

And I haven't finished even a third of my great novel.

He stands for several moments looking out over the Mexican town of Ensenada, which is beginning to bake under a mid-morning sun. He turns abruptly toward Carlotta and shouts violently,

Not one damn chapter is really finished!

What do you think of that my dearest Carlotta?

He begins to pace around the bed, increasing his anxiety. Now completely enraged with himself he again yells at Carlotta. Carlotta is used to his ravings and proceeds to bite into a large ripe papaya.

What good is all this? Where am I going?

What am I? Soon I'll be middle-aged and I've done nothing with
my life. Do you hear me?

Nothing, absolutely nothing!

Again he stops at the window, this time with his back to Carlotta—sulking. Two large palm leaves begin to sway in the light intermittent breeze, casting intricate shadows over the side of the adobe wall directly below—momentarily hypnotizing him. Then, miraculously his mood changes and he faces Carlotta.

He speaks softly.

I'm sorry, I didn't mean to shout at you that way . . .

KONRAD (to himself)

and I'm thinking about? . . .

Oh, yes here I am in a little adobe hotel by the ocean with
Carlotta—dearest Carlotta . . . only seventeen and yet Faithful
to me as a sister . . . yes that's who she is . . . my sister . . . no, no
she isn't . . .

Where is Ann?

KONRAD (to himself)

Carlotta is young, very young. She has facial features not yet
developed fully to produce that ultimate Latin beauty--straight
black hair constantly hanging over her face hiding her dark eyes.
She does have a primitive loveliness seemed to be enhanced by
her habit of going barefooted, that fascinates me, but not so much
that they are long thin feet, but that they are usually dirty long
thin feet. She is really quite tall by Mexican standards and walks
with a natural grace. I think her dark skin is inherited from an
Indian Grandmother. I have told her how I liked it when she pins
a flower in her hair. Her girlish smile has helped me through many

a troubled evening and in many ways I am very close to being in
love with you. If you only knew what I am thinking Carlotta.

VO

(Konrad narrates)

> Purple and white plains
> Graying sky
> Tinged with rust and dust
> Somewhere far, far, far
> Is a love that must
> Love, love, love—through the
> Endless wind
> Blowing, steaming, warm as a friend
> Sage so sweet, sand so soft,
> Shifting, shifting into smooth drifts
> Emotions changing, mixed being
> Tossed about
> Soon these too try to find
> Their final hue
> Such a wondrous process is
> Achieved through you

3. EXT/HOUSE—NIGHT

Evening has come to Ensenada and now a constant breeze brings the smell of the sea through the
one large window of the room. As Konrad stands looking from this window he notices two boys
below roasting something over a small fire on the rocks.

KONRAD (to himself)

How far away I have had traveled and for what purpose. I have
roamed Mexico for several months and have obtained passage on
a small freighter that is to take paper to British Honduras.

My plan had been to disembark at Progresso, Yucatan, continue by plane from Merida to Havana and from there return to Canada, but somehow my plans changed when I met Carlotta.

Every once in a while, I must convince myself I am not really in love with Carlotta but she is a great comfort to me—something, in a way, I have never known.

3. INT/ROOM—DAY

[Scene]

A fresh cement odor permeates the partially completed hotel and the newly laid tiles are covered with construction dust. Lying on his bed he could see out at the first stars appearing in the rapidly darkening sky and sounds of a dying day passes through his mind as he drifts off to sleep.

FO

FI

[Scene]

A truck rattles loudly below as it passes down the cobblestone street, awakening him with a start. Carlotta was still sleeping. Poking his head far out of the window he could see to his right over the red-tiled rooftops of the seashore town or look directly at the ocean below to his left. Not a cloud is in sight.

KONRAD (to himself)

It will be a viciously hot day as I come out onto the street the heat reflects from the white stucco of the shop frontages, causing me to catch my breath.

[Scene]

He spots an open café at the corner. While sitting on a high stool drinking a concoction of fruit juices, he decides he will walk along the fishing wharf to pass the time. The wharf is swarming with activity. He sees his friend Humberto and asks him if he could help them fish today. With a big toothy smile, Humberto motions him onto the boat. There are six other fisherman onboard and all immediately appeared to enjoy the diversion brought on by his presence. Soon they finish loading on all the gear and manage to start what sounded like a rather unreliable inboard engine that had seen its better days in the belly of a Ford truck. After a short feeble effort in reverse, the boat turns and it begins its job of chugging out to sea.

KONRAD (to himself)

Carlotta is used to my wanderings for a few days at a time so I feel free of any worldly obligations and for the first time in a long while my mind seems clear.

[Scene]

Konrad joins the others under a wide piece of canvas with brightly colored stripes. The fishermen do not talk to each other at first and a certain tension is finally broke by one of the men who offers him a banana, a small orange-colored variety that has both a sour taste followed by a slightly bitter one.

Konrad shakes his head. The choppy sea passes quickly along, flickering bright tropic sun rays causing Konrad to squint until his eyes are virtually closed. Flying fish glide from waves that are about to break, and sail from great distances before disappearing again into the warm waters of the gulf. The waves are pulled under the thirty-four foot boat and through—the propellers churning them to white foam.

One of the men; standing on the roof of the cabin holds onto a rope as if he were riding a bronco. He lowers his hand that shields his eyes and shouts. The others immediately go into action. They have sighted a large school of fish. The boat is steered to port in a wide sweeping arc and then began dumping overboard the neatly folded net. Konrad joins in, but soon the immediate thrill of excitement turns into hard work. His lean arms were unaccustomed to the strenuous effort of pulling in the heavy wet net.

After several hours of throwing and pulling the net in the hot sun, Konrad's dark tan begins to show a deeper reddish tinge. The water has soon turned to a huge smooth metallic gray plate that rolls quietly by. The boat slaps up and down ever so slightly in the unusually calm waters as the men shovel ice onto the catch, burying layer upon layer of fish.

Konrad sheds his trousers and jumps into the cooling sea. The fishermen appear to take vicarious delight in seeing him sooth his sun-scorched back as he swims like a wallowing walrus. They yell, jokingly, that the sharks will get him, but he simply laughs along with them. Two hours later it is beginning to get dark. Several lights shine from the nearby coast.

A slight breeze turn stronger and black clouds race overhead. The wind continues to rise and soon large raindrops pelt down. The sea becomes a swarming mass that began tossing the craft about. The engine will not start. The boat is coming dangerously close to the coastal rocks. Moments later it strikes ground on a sandy cove and jerks violently to starboard, tossing three of the crew and Konrad into the sea. The others leap overboard. All stagger to shore and through the torrents of rain, make their way along a path to a straw-roofed house of a peasant farmer.

The doorway has been made for shorter people and Konrad finds it necessary to stoop as he stumbles into the one-room adobe house. He wipes the rain, which drips from his hair over his face, and peers through the smoke-filled room. A table is in the center of the room and in one corner is an old-fashioned iron bed from which two small children stare, awakened and frightened by the many new voices. A chicken flaps across the dirt floor.

The fisherman, make appropriate greetings and then begin to place small fish into a fire. Konrad is invited to sit on the table. Soon after, the farmer takes a stick and rakes the blackened fish from the coals. He proceeds to hand one to Konrad being the guest. The others began breaking open the burnt fish and picking out the non-burnt inner steaming white meat with their teeth. He copies them and finds the fish meat burning hot but tasty. The smoke hangs thick and the more he rubs his eyes the more they hurt. But soon an overwhelming urge to sleep makes him curl up on top of the table and moments later he is fast asleep—to dream....

FO

VO

        KONRAD (Konrad narrates/background is a mosaic of color)

    I am thinking of someone but I cannot quite visualize her.
    Across a room
    On an evening of delight
    My sight fell upon
    Beauty sweet and bright
    That beauty augmented by autumn leaves

Became a glow that nights did breath
The mosaic of color
That reflected in her face
Caused all of the spectra to embrace
The light and shadows
Of her feminine grace
I danced with her soul one night
So tenderly, so pale in the dim moonlight
Yet blazing it was
Fluorescing amidst the beaming starlight
Her warmth and smile
To one such as I
Merely created emotion, while
One second's possession of her heart
A whirl to my own it would impart
That beauty augmented by autumn leave
Became a glow that cold nights did breathe
The mosaic of color
That reflected in her face
Caused all the spectra to embrace
The light and shadows
Of her feminine grace

FO

FI

4. EX/BEACH—DAY

                    KONRAD (to himself)

The clean smell of the sea came to his nose.

[Scene]

No one was in the room. Outside Konrad could see men down at the beach. The boat was being refloated and then was anchored about thirty yards off the shore, apparently undamaged. He is greeted with a cheer from the crew, including a bit of razzing for waking after everyone else. The fishermen then gather around a driftwood fire with the flames licking around a large tin can. A dip of a big spoon brings forth a huge hunk of barracuda with rice which is being boiled with pieces of red pepper. Several black vultures arrogantly and awkwardly come forth like begging dogs. They attempt to scare them away but this only makes them flap loudly. They realign themselves a few feet away and soon are back at their original stations.

5. EXT/HOUSE—DAY

Konrad finds himself waving his arms wildly and screaming at the vultures, and . . . begins yelling for Carlotta.

KONRAD

Carlotta, Carlotta . . . Oh where are you?

I have been dreaming about fishing with our friend Humberto and vultures and . . . bring me some rum, just a little please, I'm so groggy.

Konrad walks out onto the veranda. A piece of paper is being tossed around by the wind. He becomes hypnotized by its erratic behavior. At first it seems to be dancing gaily—being lifted lightly and falling gently. But then soon it is dashed violently against the banister and sits there for some moments, constrained and confined, seemingly not being allowed to be free to express itself. Finally it slips down to the floor of the porch. Konrad sees his life being reflected in these few moments and begins to feel dejected.

FO

FI

6. EXT/PARISIAN PARK—DAY

[Scene]

The sun blazed off the noon waters—drowning Konrad in thoughts, images begin to appear—flickering in the hot sun—like an old movie . . . a man steps from the entrance of a small hotel in the Place Pigalle sector of Paris. He turns left and walks slowly to the corner. As he strolls along he feels his depression begin to lift for it is a fine autumn morning. He goes up the block and crosses over to the midway and then heads for his usual bench.

The chill air causes him to pull his scarf under his chin. Then he reaches into his coat pocket and draws out a small bag full of crumbs. Three pigeons immediately flutter near and, as he began tossing crumbs, he realizes the strange melancholic feeling is beginning to return. It was something alien, yet something not—something on a frosty night in moon-drenched field. He could almost remember but not quite and then it vanishes.

Again it appears and he clearly sees a field full of dry matted grass bathed in silver light, surrounded by rotting oak trees squeaking in the wind. Overhead honking geese pass across the moon's face and on through the icy black sky. But he can not identify or assign these visions as to time and places.

In the morning he felt weak. However, his recollection of the field does not make him depressed, but still leaves him feeling very alone and abandoned. There is an absent look on his face and a disheveled appearance like that of a person caught in an economic depression, standing in line for their rations. The view of the field returns.

The sun sets behind the dense trees near the edge of the field and the wind is sinister and cold. The light became feeble as the first star glimmers between fast moving low dark clouds overhead. It is a strange coldness, empty and silent. He leans over to pick up one of the crumbs to toss to a sparrow that has been an unsuccessful competitor. The man might have easily been mistaken for a person of fifty and the rather ill-fitting brownish-black coat he wares do little to alleviate this impression. Three boys run by the bench, yelling as they chase each other on past a large old fountain full of dry leaves.

Again his thoughts return to the haunting field. This time it is late afternoon and he can hear the call of a crow on a nearby woodshed. Against the horizon, a swirl of smoke is rising. A distant howl of a hound is followed first by the hooting of an owl as evening approaches and then by voices, far away, of children playing. He asked himself—can these be parts of his life he has forgotten? Small trucks, taxis, and other cars rattle by, honking at each other, racing wildly down the cobbled street in front of him, but he does not notice them.

Eventually the activity of the pigeons drew his attention. The sun's rays begin to filter through the barren branches of the thin chestnut trees behind the bench. The passing cars swirl the dead leaves around the man's legs as the pigeons coo and peck at his feet. A tear appears and passes over his cheek, running to the corner of his mouth. He wipes it away, closes his eyes, and turns his face into the warm sun, which is beginning to break the early morning chill. The branches cast a web of shadows that sway slightly to and fro over the bench.

He thinks to himself. He can bear these days of loneliness if he can only have someone to remember. A pigeon glides near, abruptly turns and perches upon the back of the bench beside him. He reaches into the bag. All the crumbs are gone. Not far away a nun approaches a bench on the other side and sits down. Suddenly wings explode around him in all directions and the pigeons flap loudly to join the others already feeding around the nun. The man sits on the bench, immobile and stares out at traffic....

FO

FI

7. INT/HOUSE—DAY

KONRAD

Carlotta, was I ever in Paris?

Konrad reaches out and holds her and afterwards she hands him a half glass of rum.

CARLOTTA

No, my darling. I don't think so. Maybe before, before many years
ago, maybe.

She holds his hand tightly.

You have been ill now for many weeks.

The doctors in Ensenada told her he seems mentally exhausted.

CARLOTTA (to herself)

I want to take care of Konrad. He is fascinating to me. I will make
him happy again.

Konrad's mind wanders to his boyhood days....

VO (A Spanish speaking voice)

¿Donde Estaba Las Lucie'rnagas?

Cuando ere un muchacho
Casaba las lucie'rnagas
¿Perodo'nde?...En el prado?
¿En que' noche basamico de
Verano corri's y casaba
Las lucie'rnagas?
¡O, Dio! No puedo recorder.
Ahora ando abajo las sendas
Las sendas parezco he sabido antes
Como si hube dado un paso
Su polvo
Durante los tiempos mas quietos
Hace muchos edads.
El tiempo, lo siento
Por todas partes de mi'
Confudiendo, extendiendo, girando
Lentamente—
Como alguna vi'a la'ctea giante
Silenciosa.
¡Yo pierdo! Querido Dio, yo pierdo.
Por favor. Au'ydame a encontrar lucie'rnagas otra vez

[Note; Dubbing: Where were the fireflies? When I was a boy I would chase the fireflies. But where?
What meadow? On that balmy night of summer did I run and hunt the fireflies? Oh, God! I cannot
remember. Now I walk along the path. A path, it seems, I have walked before as if I had walked

177

upon its dust, during a time more tranquil many ages ago. A time, somewhere, everywhere mixing, extending, revolving slowly, as some silent giant galaxy. I'm lost! Dear God, I'm lost. Please, help me find the fireflies again.]

1. EXT/HOUSE—DAY

Konrad sees blurred mirage-like images, as if a stage play is being performed before him...

FI

KONRAD (to himself)

[Scene]

> A vision comes to me. It begins with multifaceted small rocks, ones that can be used for pathways. Each rock has its own colors. That one has orange on one face and on the adjacent side a slightly different hue, ocher, I believe. As a collection these pebbles give rise to a particular narrow path. It is summertime. I can actually see it. It is so real. It is very hot. There is a path that becomes a triangle. I see it clearly now, in an early afternoon sun. It is real! At one point of the triangle is a small chapel where nuns are praying. Near another corner lies a small building with several bedroom quarters for novices. The remaining corner of the triangle broadens forming white steps that lead to a tiny gazebo. The interior of the triangle is embedded with hundreds of rose bushes, which suffocates the mind with all of its colors. Two figures are bent near one of the corners—one standing, one kneeling. Both are pruning the rose bushes.

PAPA

Your mind seems preoccupied small one.

He is the older of the two, a man of some forty years. He stares momentarily into the sun and then wipes his brow with an oversized handkerchief.

RAUL

I'm thinking how pretty the new novice is.

Raul has black curly hair and is small for a seventeen year old.

Don't you think she is pretty, Papa?

PAPA

I never noticed, and you shouldn't be noticing either.

RAUL

Why not, Papa?

PAPA

She's going to marry Jesus.

RAUL (to himself)

She's still pretty.

ANITA (to herself)

I am twenty and have been corralled by incessant, but subtle praises. Most of these praises are also heard by the ears of her close friends, week after week, day after day. Of course, I will become a nun. What else would I dare to become?

FO

FI

[Scene]

Anita admires Sister Superior Margarita's habit. It is a "Poor Clare" five-piece version of the Franciscan habit, with its white under-veil and black over-veil, form-fitting coif, and a large white guimpe. Anita's tunic has no scapular overlay and is all grey, with a rope belt around her waist. Without the stiff white crown band it looks more like the Carmelite habit than a Franciscan Sisters of Saint Bartholomew habit.

ANITA (to herself)

Actually, I feel that I appear more like a monk than a nun.

KONRAD (typing)

Her "roundish" face with "cream and peaches" complexion makes her a lovely looking girl. The full figure is a reflection of her healthy childhood. She must have been raised on a small farm just a short distance from Salamanca.

[Scene]

When Raul works the chapel corner of the triangle he can hear the murmuring of prayer through the windows. The noonday bells begin ringing, signaling the end to morning vespers. The vesper time has to be changed from the usual evening hours in the winter, because the chapel is still too hot. In the early morning it remains just tolerable throughout the summer.

A small flock of white pigeons rise from the bell tower and soar into the heights over the rose garden below whenever the bells toll. Raul wishes he could be a pigeon; if for only one flight, to see the roses he only knows by toiling on his knees. He maneuvers over where his work can be nearer the entrance of the chapel. In this way he can be able to see Anita, when she leaves the chapel for her siesta.

On the day of her arrival at the nunnery she falls over Raul's outstretched leg as he is toiling in the thick rose bushes. They come face to face when Raul instinctively rolls over. Anita blushes as she picked herself up and both begin apologizing.

FO

FI

2. INT/ANITA'S BED—NIGHT

Raul's image taunts her and at daybreak he is in her first thoughts.

[Later]

3. EXT/ROSE GARDEN—DAY

As weeks pass, they exchange glances. Anita allows Raul to walk closely behind her. She somehow feels comforted by his presence.

INT/CHAPEL-DAY

But now she finds it necessary to go to confession to atone for her thoughts. Anita's mind is becoming more and more filled with conflict. She is aware of her potential heretic soul, but that was why she has to come to the nunnery, to save herself from damnation. Anita walks ever so slowly through the arched walkways of the cloister.

These walkways are built around the backyard of the chapel. The walkway itself is surrounded by a low flat stone wall covered by dark ivy. Here she prays amongst the wild rose vines cascading above from the arcades. The chapel has its adjacent cheerful, formal rose garden. To the north looms a medieval monastic abbey, gloomy and deteriorating.

KONRAD (typing)

> Some of the townspeople say they heard the cries of the
> beguinages—women who have chosen to live the life of abstinence
> and solitude until their abolition was decreed in the year 1312.

4. EXT/ANITA'S ROOM—NIGHT

Anita feels particularly drained and after blowing her candle out, she begins to think of the huge grey monastery with its immense tower. Soon she is dreaming, dreaming of smearing great gobs of dark red lipstick onto her cheeks and forehead.

5. EXT/MONASTERY—NIGHT

She then begins running, stumbling barefoot along the rough stones on the road that leads to the hilltop monastery lit by flickering lightning from an oncoming storm. The monastery looks cruel and ugly. The wind begins tearing at her habit.

FO

FI

6. INT/ANITA'S ROOM—NIGHT

Anita awakes in a sweat and puts on a cape over her white nightshirt and goes out onto the grassy knoll just outside the bunkhouse. The crickets are loud. She walks barefoot over to the lot just south of the chapel. Spidery webs of shadows play upon the side of the chapel wall from the night zephyrs. Anita begins to pray.

FO

FI

7. INT/RAUL'S BEDROOM—NIGHT

Raul sees Anita from his room passing along the garden path in the moonlight.

8. EXT/GAZEBO—NIGHT

They meet at the gazebo. They look forward upon the moonlit path, then gaze together at the stars, and then stare into each other's eyes. His hand touches hers. They hold hands for a fleeting moment and then part without speaking a word.

[Two days later]

Increasingly hot weather passes before Raul sees Anita again. The heat is stifling. Breathing the hot air makes the body burst into sweat. The sun bares down on the roses.

9. EXT/ROSE GARDEN—DAY

Anita comes down the path toward the novice's bunkhouse at the third corner of the triangle. She catches Raul's eye upon her and soon Raul, mesmerized, follows her to the bunkhouse.

10. INT/ANITA'S ROOM

The adobe walls are cracked and small shreds of yellow straw are imbedded near the surface glistening in the noon sun. Raul steps gently upon the white stone threshold. Next he enters quietly into the dark hallway, turning to follow Anita. Since the door is not closed behind her, he passes into the small bedroom with its plain walls. The only adornments present are a miniature statue of the Virgin Mary, which stands on a small table beside the rough-hewn bunk bed, and a wooden carving of Christ upon the cross that made a large-angled shadow over the whitewashed plaster wall.

> KONRAD (to himself)
>
> The total image is reminiscent of an Albrecht Dürer wood-block print done in sepia.

11. INT/ANITA'S ROOM—DAY

Anita's soft brown eyes are staring deeply into his. Her urges are released. She let out a moan of passion as Raul's head arches back.

FO

FI

12. INT/ANITA'S ROOM—NIGHT

Anita begins to sleep fitfully.

> ANITA (to herself)
>
> I will put on makeup. I feel a compulsion, drawing me out of this room and I will flow through the door and out onto the monastery road.

She passes over the rough stones once again, only this time her feet hurt . . . disrobing, now running nude through the rain. There is lightning. She goes onward toward the monastery summit, climbing over gate stones and into the entrance, which over the years has become a large dark hole.

FO

FI

13. EXT/ROSE GARDEN—DAY

Raul thinks he hears angels singing in the chapel the next morning. Their close harmonic high tones pass over the rose garden and lift out into the afternoon skies. Anita is missing from the prayer session.

[Later]

Anita's body is found deep in the interior depths of the old monastery.

FO

FI

KONRAD (to himself)

VO (Konrad typing)

> A vision comes to me. It begins with multifaceted small rocks, ones that can be used for pathways. Each rock has its own colors. That one has on one face, orange, and on the adjacent side a slightly different hue, I believe it is ocher.
>
> As a collection these pebbles give rise to a particular narrow path. The vision is in summer. I can actually see it. It is so real. It is very hot. The path becomes a rectangle. At one point of the rectangle is a small chapel where nuns are praying.

Near another corner lies a small building having several bedroom quarters for novices. Still another corner of the rectangle broadens, becoming white steps leading to a tiny gazebo. On the remaining corner the roses are dying and appear like wilted flowers in a Maurice de Vlaminck painting . . . and with these the garden is now complete.

14. EXT/ KONRAD'S HOUSE—DAY

Konrad's eyes are blurring as he looks too long into the bright light.

> KONRAD (to himself)

I am trying to see something, something past the light into another time.

> KONRAD

Carlotta, did you enjoy the bullfight yesterday?

> CARLOTTA

Yes, it was thrilling. I like it when you take me to the fiestas.

> CARLOTTA (to herself)

I feel so sorry for him. He has not taken me anywhere for weeks and we have not seen a bullfight for many months. It is his wife who has taken him years ago.

FI

> KONRAD (to himself)

Glancing at her out of the corner of my eye, I can see she is definitely apprehensive. This is her first attendance at a bullfight. What should I expect? I thought at least I would get to see the first bull killed.

[Scene]

The arena is magnificent, teeming with a profusion of colors, enough to suffocate the imagination. Yet there pervades an awesome feeling of potential death. It is a special occasion and the President steps into his seat high above us. A roar of cheers comes forth as to keep the possibility of a matador dying from entering one's mind. A Mexican sits beside two beer bottles in front of us and is in a festive mood and continually squeezes the goatskin, shooting a stream of wine onto his palate.

The bull enters and soon the picador has placed the pic deep into its shoulder. The blood streams over the shiny hair. Torero Manelo Bienvanidata enters from our left. My digestion of clams from Paella Valenciana stops. The brute of a bull, black, mean and snorting, crashes into the padded horse, tipping it and his caballero to the ground. A deft jab of its horns into the exposed belly of the horse produced a partial evisceration. The game was on!

Soon with workhorses and chains, the carcass is dragged across the dirt and through the gateway, leaving a plowed trail behind. The bull charges again. This time a keen veronica from Manelo subdues the mass to its knees. Another and another pass. Artistry, pure artistry with its cape. The crowd roared its approval. Close, closer with each pass. Then suddenly a toss and a ragdoll-like figure is in the air. The bull has wet its horns revengefully. The man is reduced in the moment to a mere half-living mortal. The spectators rise to their feet. Silence.

Four attendants rush out and carry the brave man above them, his arms dangling puppet-like at his sides, with a blood-smeared face. But within a few minutes he staggers back into the arena with a mulatto. The crowd goes hysterical. The sword is revealed, quickly aimed, and inserted. Great heaving begins and a voluminous vomit of blood gushes forth, splattering a thick foamy spray from the dilated nostrils of the huge beast. The bull sways, then goes over on his side, kicking.

FO

FI

15. EXT/KONRAD'S HOUSE—DAY

[Later that afternoon]

KONRAD (to himself)

I feel strong enough to go out onto the veranda again and write.

Three violet-headed colibri hum about the tormpeta and campanilla blossoms as a questral surveys the veranda from the eucalyptus tree. The words flow ever so easily. I will work on two separate works, one will be a novel, The Hummingbird. He begins to type as the sun burns down on his back...

FI

23 INT/RESTAURANT—DAY

KONRAD (typing)

VO

The heat baked the clay buildings like a Dutch brick oven. This was Tangier in August. The sweat beaded on the man's forehead. He appeared to be a typical camera-dangling tourist. As he looked out the open window of the restaurant, he argued with himself as to whether he really was enjoying the black pepper sauce that the waiter had just poured on the rice. Beyond him were the crowded flat-topped houses that formed a mosaic of rectangular blocks of subtle beiges, yellows and off-whites. Immediately below him he could see a rooftop surrounded by high walls.

16. EXT/HOUSE ROOF—DAY

[Scene]

A clothes line stretched across from the doorway opening onto the roof area. A boy, cloaked in a brown kaftan, stepped from the doorway and a cat jumped from the perch on top of the wall. The man grappled for his expensive camera. As he cocked the shutter he imagined himself as a boy...

THE MAN (to himself)

Ben Ralem had just come from wandering about the stalls in the bazaar on his way home from smoking kef with Abdullah, his close friend.

The Moroccan boy looked up. The man quickly jerked his glance back to the steeping teapot sitting before him. The boy could see a man wearing sunglasses and a fine suit sitting near an open window directly above. He dreamed of such life . . .

THE BOY (to himself)

He was leaving a tip, several dirhams, from a large wad of folded money . . . stepping down the stairway and into his black limousine . . . he would leave for the airport for he must catch the 13:30 flight for Lisbon where the Belgian finance minister is to meet him.

17. INT/RESTAURANT—DAY

The man looked down on the rooftop.

18. EXT/ROOFTOP—DAY

The boy turned quickly, stumbling over the cat. He had almost been caught staring at the foreigner.

19. INT/RESTAURANT—DAY

The man longed to be Ralem, a boy with no worries. He dreaded the next few days. When he got back to New York, he would meet his wife at the lawyer's office to finalize their divorce . . .

THE MAN (to himself)

He and Abdullah would get together this evening

and find a young goat to roast.

The boy felt sad.

THE BOY (to himself)

I have to go to class tomorrow at the School of Popular Arts. Father makes me learn plaster craft and yet I would rather not . . . the man in the fine suit enters the yacht club and walks over to the bar. The bartender speaks first, "Well, hello, Mr. Smith. Have you been away? I haven't seen you in some time." The man replies, "You're right. I've just come back from Lisbon. Do you know if Peter has been around? We were going to enter the race next week."

A woman called loudly from inside the doorway. The boy turned and went inside.

20. EXT/OUTSIDE OF RESTAURANT—DAY

The bus driver announced the resumption of the tour. The man left the table to join the line of people shuffling back onto the sight-seeing bus....

FO

FI

21. INT/KONRAD'S HOUSE—DAY

Konrad sits back—his mind exhausted.

[Scene]

The sun sets over the hill to the north and the hot beach breeze begins to cool.

[The following day]

KONRAD (to himself)

I feel good and although it is raining heavily I have decided to see my publisher in San Diego.

Konrad chokes slightly, drinking freshly squeezed tart orange juice as he asks Carlotta to drive him to the bus station and added that he should be back late tomorrow evening. He tells her to be a good girl and gave her some money to do some shopping while she was in town. Konrad kisses Carlotta gently on the cheek and slowly climbs aboard the bus to San Diego.

22. INT/BUS—NIGHT

The sign reads: NO SMOKING EXCEPT IN THE LAST THREE ROWS. In the rear, however, the more prevalent odor is the smell of whiskey. A telltale bottle slides across the floor as the bus rounds a curve, as it speeds onward towards a rising moon. The wheels hum. Distant lights from a desert home orbit slowly together and then as heavenly bodies with unequal but predictable motions, separate again. A fat, fortyish woman, whose slovenly legs hang over the arm rest of the rear sear, brake the short period of silence, waking several passengers from their fitful doze with a loud,

WOMAN ON BUS

> "Well, I left three husbands behind—one dead, one divorced, and
> one god damn unfaithful mutt!"

Across the aisle a sleepy head nods, reluctantly acknowledging her attempt at conversation but hoping not to prompt any continuation. Her loud grating voice join is joined by the rasping noise of the sliding whiskey bottle and seems to be in concert with the background drone of the motor. The toilet door is ajar to swing with the movement of the bus, slams twice before clicking itself shut. A release of the airbrakes heralds a "rest" stop.

The glare of overhead lights floods the minds of the captive passengers to a cup of unwanted coffee. Climbing aboard like returning slaves from a pyramid building site, the travelers again prepare for a fitful wink of sleep, and the bus lurches forward. A man with a weary face, lonely and quite willing to join in a chat now, sits across from the fat woman.

MAN ON BUS

> I'm headed for Barstow, California. Got a friend there. He's gonna
> give me a job.

Slight tearing in his wind-burnt eyes sparkle for an instant in the light of a passing car.

> I had no work for a long time.

The fat woman says nothing. Her head bends onto her knees, snoring deep and drunk. Up front large drops of rain begin to splatter heavily on the windshield as the wipers swish monotonously.

The bus roars on, the empty whisky bottle slides back across the floor. Konrad awakes. The sign outside reads TIJUANA.

In front of him he sees just above the seat back the head of a young girl who must have gotten on while he was asleep. Crawling all over the seat across the aisle from her, as if preparing for a Mount Everest climb, are two much smaller children. A voice rings out loud and clear.

GIRL ON BUS

You get your asses down on the seat!

KONRAD (to himself)

Apparently she has to take care of her younger brother and sister.
Either the parents are not with them or possibly they are seated
elsewhere.

A strike as lightning fast as a rattlesnake's, she has slapped the wide-eyed, about-to-cry little girl—but no tears. I am impressed. It seems they are used to severe discipline but venture a try at things anyway, though courageous if caught. At the next stop Konrad notices the girl as she steps across the aisle. She is pregnant! This young girl, who does not appear to Konrad to be more than sixteen, is obviously the mother of these one-and two-year-old tots. Konrad stares at them. The two-year-old girl looks into Konrad's face.

TWO YEAR OLD TOT

Daddy.

The young mother speaks, quite resigned to life's fate.

MOTHER/GIRL

He's not your daddy. Your daddy is in jail—where he usually is.

They arrive in south San Diego. The rain has ended and a setting sun manages to flicker through the broken clouds near the horizon into Konrad's face as the bus passes by the city's buildings. The bus turns into the downtown station.

23. EXT/CAB—DAY

Konrad catches a cab. It is getting late. He arrives just in time at Pacific Publishers. Mr. Murray is to leave in twenty minutes for home to get ready for a dinner party that evening.

24. INT/MURRAY'S OFFICE

MURRAY

Well, well, Konrad—it's about time you showed up. I have reason to be peeved.

Konrad has not been in touch for several months.

KONRAD (to himself)

Murray always strikes me as being a walrus of sorts with his bushy mustache and eyebrows and round face and body. His buck teeth could even pass for tusks. But I respect Murray's long experience with the written word and I will never let this walrus notion interfere with the wisdom of Murray's criticisms. Murray's grumblings begin.

MURRAY

I looked over that latest manuscript of the Hummingbird plot and to be perfectly candid with you, the last part of the plot is weak and meaningless. That section where the research physiologist is doing those experiments with a pet hummingbird on cellular energy needs something or whatever—what is this, a textbook or a novel? Really now—the rest of that section, on the other hand is quite acceptable, where he meets Ann in Lima at the science convention on metabolism and something.

KONRAD (to himself)

The conversation seems to be rather one-sided. I am beginning to feel somewhat dejected. But I am no novice and have been through many of these critiquing sessions before and somehow they don't seem to bother me anymore.

FO

[Over the speaker system.]

Mr. Konrad Martin to the ticket counter.

As he approached the ticket area he noticed a strikingly handsome young lady in a green suit.

KONRAD

Yes, I'm Mr. Martin (to the ticket agent)

ADELE

Oh, I'm the one asking for you.

KONRAD (to himself)

It's the lady in green.

ADELE

My name is Adele. I'm a close friend of Murray. I've come to invite you to the dinner party this evening. We'd love to have you.

KONRAD

Well, I guess I could stay one more day. I'd like to make a phone call to someone back in Ensenada.

ADELE

Oh, why don't you call from Murray's place or better still since we'll actually be driving to where the party will be, you could phone them from there, alright?

                    KONRAD (to himself)

Adele wairs her clothing with class, presenting an excellent
posture. She reminds me of the women in fashion magazines who
model business suits. Her presumably grey-brown hair is short
and neat and her green eyes are intense, matching her outfit. Her
complexion is pale and perfect—she has the Garbo look.

While they drive through the streets of San Diego, Konrad begins to write in his mind . . .

FI

25. EXT/CAR—DAY

                    KONRAD (to himself)

[Scene]

        Yellows of the dunes, scruffy sheep, dull orange towers of sand,
        shimmering air blue in the moonlight, ornately painted doors of
        egg blue and bright rust with worn wooden latches, rose-colored
        clouds drifting lightly toward the unending horizon, nests of
        porches jutting from adobe apartments, shop shuttered, men in
        long white robes, sands shifting, ridges forming shadows, haughty
        stately camels crunching thorn tree limbs, fig palm sprays swaying,
        sand ripples, goat-hair tents and gabwa strong coffee, prayer
        mats and rugs, Allah Akbar chants, thick sugary tea, ghutras
        red, ghutras white, ghutras hanging near leathery faces held in
        place by black agal cords, shaggy black-haired Nubian goats with
        long white ears hanging horizontal slit yellow eyes, daggers in
        scabbards of silver filigree, souks stuffed with dangling chains of
        gold, opaque turquoise and aquamarine waters of the sea, Arabian
        crows, overhead, hawks and vultures soaring in the hot winds, the
        sun melting back into the cool sands of evening.

A jeep made its way through the crowded narrow street and then passed through the huge gateway of the city of Sana. A military policeman and an air force officer rode in the back seat. The officer looked back at that arch as if trying to see in to the past. He remembered that day. The hot air had been almost too hot to breath. Major Charles Henson, an officer of the United States Air Force,

HENSON

You understand, Cynthia, I got reassigned to the base in Yemen because of trouble with a guerilla movement that has recently intensified here. But, last week I have obtained permission to bring you to the base. And now here you are beside me.

The canvas-covered jeep careens around the curve, and a dust cloud follows as though it were the vapor trail of a strato-jet. Major Henson looks over and smiles nervously and squeezes his wife's hand in a desperate gesture to assure her that everything would be alright. Cynthia Henson, the epitome of charm and femininity, had been protected all her life. She has a certain reserved manner befitting of her family background.

Her thirty-nine years has not, thus far, left her unattractive. The hot winds lifts the sand into their faces, and Mrs. Henson is soon attempting to clear the grittiness accumulating between her teeth by spitting as politely as possible. Major Henson nervously twists his distinguished looking moustache.

Suddenly, he leans forward pointing to the side of the cliff on his side and yells something to the driver. She didn't realize their ploy to divert her attention at that particular moment had failed, for she notices on her side near the road's edge several bodies of men—men without heads! In a repulsive jerk she turns to the direction Charles was pointing, and as he looks around, he shouts to her that he has just seen a gazelle. They stop about ten miles from Sana to drink the warm water from a canister before finishing the journey that had started from the seaport of Aden.

The high-walled town of Sana is directly ahead, but the corporal steers to the left on what is little more than a goat path. It will be several days before Cynthia Henson will learn the reason for not entering through the main entrance. There the heads of the headless bodies of guerillas hang from the archway.

The little room they will have this night is comparatively luxurious to the dirty three-room flat in which they would eventually stay since they would have to live off the base. All night he worries. He will have to tell her that even boiled water cannot be drunk; that the reason he shook everything he picked off the floor is to get rid of many scorpions; that he himself has recently been bitten by one and had to be rushed to a nearby army base where a Polish doctor had injected an antitoxin into his rapidly swelling arm. Could he tell her of last week's gang raping of a native girl? This is surely sheer madness on his part to bring his wife here.

Recently his depressed state has made his mind wander, and this had frightened him. He had convinced himself there are no alternatives. He still cannot conceive of his wife's change over these last few months. Not only did she learn to cope with the arduous, barren life, she thrives in it, becoming outgoing, loud, and constantly laughing. Although she knew her husband is madly jealous, she dances with anyone and everyone at the base "get-togethers." Then she begins to seek even more entertainment outside the base. Some nights he finds her at the cabaret filled with its blue haze of spice smelling kef. She wildly flirts with the locals and ends up sprawled out on the floor "doped to the gills." And finally she tells him she is going to leave him and run off with Armand, the seventeen year old who attends the café.

He goes to the bureau drawer for the pistol and stops her insane behavior forever.... It has all been a terrible nightmare and he is having difficulty in understanding what point of this nightmare he was in . . . déjà vu! His thoughts cycle again and again! He looks down at his handcuffs, then out onto the dusty road, that same road... and now here she is beside him. The canvas-covered jeep careens around the curve and a dust cloud follows as though it were a vapor trail of a strato-jet. He looks over and smiles nervously and squeezes his wife's hand, in a desperate gesture to assure her that everything would be all right....

FI

26. EXT/YACHT—NIGHT

ADELE

Here we are.

Adele looks into Konrad's face for a surprised look.

KONRAD

Terrific.

KONRAD (to himself)

I think Adele might be surprised had she known that I have been in Yemen moments before.

They stop on the wharf in front of a small yacht.

ADELE

We rented the yacht for the evening and someone is going to drive Murray here a little later and we'll give him a surprise party on it—great idea?

Konrad was beginning to remember a yacht party somewhere in the Mediterranean . . . somewhere in his mind . . . there had been a yacht party . . .

27. EXT/YACHT—NIGHT

KONRAD

It's a beautiful yacht.

Konrad steps aboard. Adele looks back flirtatiously.

KONRAD (to himself)

I will write a letter to Ann that can be used in the Hummingbird plot....

Dear Ann,

No problems, I am alright. I'm going to make it, by God, somehow. Already a whole twelve hours since I left the island and I am looking back to the island. It isn't the island that has me crying, it's you that has me crying so hard, to show the world what you mean to me. The island is gone. You're gone. Was I about to lose control? The next island is dead ahead....

Love, Konrad

KONRAD (to himself)

Yes, I will go to San Diego to see Ann . . . Adele ...leave Ann...

VO

Burning the skies
The roar of the wind and
Waves of love
The catastrophe of life
A love lurking
On the rocks of destruction
Before even knowing
Of itself and its greatness
The morphine of reality
The life-beat of drums
The smoke of basic desires
Smoldering into sparks
Of frustration
Gasping as of drowning
In a sea of sensations
Gasping in dream worlds
Searching for you
Screaming in the midnight air
Running through time itself
Where, where—I've lost you
The mad dreams of a lover

28. INT/YACHT—NIGHT

KONRAD (to himself)

Was he in love with Adele? Of course not. I've just met her. I listened to my mind, but my attention is on the sounds around me.

[Scene]

The tinkling of cocktail glasses, sporadic laughter, drowning mumbling conversation, and the rare creaking from the walnut interior of the boat as it rocked lightly in the evening waves coming into the bay dock area. The party is in full swing. Murray has arrived and is enjoying himself immensely—a long-needed rest for the workaholic inside. Konrad is learning more about Adele—a thirty-year-old aggressive and very attractive woman.

He could easily observe and listen to his and her mind at once, somehow. That is how his mind had been working recently. She had been an assistant professor of English at the University of Auckland before meeting Murray on one of his junkets. The cocktails are flowing and soon Adele and Konrad are in an intellectual argument on Ovid's Metamorphosis.

At times they seem to be speaking Latin—"No, both Cadmus and his wife were changed to snakes . . . Num sacer ille mea traiectus cuspide serpens ..." but soon they are on firmer ground, at least she was, discussing Beowulf and Spencer's Faerie Queens. The discussion comes to an end once Konrad discusses his notion of the evolution of biospheres, like planet Earth, from imperfections in the space-time continuum that cause turbulences, eddies, thermodynamic aggregations and the formation of atoms—but that the culmination of biospheres is to create systems that have introspection such as humans that know they exist making the pleasure principle that control humans something that could be experienced.

Adele suggest that the universe is so big and biologically evolutionary places so small, that it was irrelevant. Konrad volleys that he believes that biospheres are light years apart so that the imperfect biospheres cannot contaminate good systems. Adele counters with a laugh and ponders whether or not the Earth is a good or bad biosphere. At that point Konrad is already on the Greek-Bulgarian border....

FI

KONRAD (to himself)

29. EXT/TRAIN—DAY

There had been quite a delay and I leaned out of the train window just in time to notice two policemen pushing a man inside of the immigration office of the train station. Moments later I hear that two Germans have attempted to smuggle a bomb to Greek student revolutionaries. I begin to formulate the plot as I look over at Vasiliki, jotting down my notes. Medical student Vasiliki: friendship struck in Skopje, train arrives at Greek border town of Idomeni, later find Vasiliki attempts assassination in Athens—she really is a revolutionary... Glancing up for a moment, I noticed Vasiliki smiling at me and I feel that I had indeed found a good friend. She is a surgeon, returning from her studies in the United States via Paris to her home in Athens. We only met hours earlier when she boarded in Skopje where she was visiting friends. I continued to write. Suddenly a uniformed man looms over me, asking for my passport.

UNIFORMED MAN

(Opening it) Your name is Konrad Martin?

KONRAD

That is correct.

Taking the notebook from my hands, he reads quickly, a stern expression coming to his face.

UNIFORMED MAN

What are these?

KONRAD

These are notes I've jotted down just few moments ago. I'm a writer. I must insist these are personal; you have no right to read them. Give them back, please.

He did not move, but with a serious expression and deepening voice coldly replied,

UNIFORMED MAN

And I take it this is your Greek friend Vasiliki?

There was death-like silence before he continued,

You two must come with me.

I am detained for several hours for questioning but it is nearly a year before I learn about my friend Vasiliki. While visiting in Kragujevae, I see in a Belgrade newspaper an article about a woman medical instructor, Dr. Vasiliki Kokkinos, who had been executed for being the instigator of a student uprising against the government at the University of Athens.

30. INT/YACHT—NIGHT

MURRY

I say there Konrad, are you all right?

KONRAD

Oh, oh yes, I'm doing fine. Great party, thanks for having me. He and Adele, along with an assistant publisher of the newspaper in Santa Cruz, Bolivia—El Tiempo, get into an intense argument on Catholicism and Konrad's mind drifts far off into a monastery....

FI

31. INT/MONASTERY—DAY

The traveler has not taken a cold shower since his Army days, the water heater has refused to work for years in the old monastery near Madrid. So, rationalizing that cold water is invigorating, he proceeds to get ready for breakfast. As a visitor he is allowed to have breakfast at one end of the huge dining hall. Here he is served something besides three sardines and an orange.

> MONK

> Good morning to you, sir. Are you enjoying your stay with us? I
> hope our beds are not too hard for you?

As the missionary speaks he has a habit of wringing his hands together as if he are constantly washing away his sins.

> VISITOR

> The beds are fine—too fine.

> MONK

> What do you mean?

> VISITOR

> (Half-jokingly), I mean that you have gone into the ways of
> materialism, Father.

The Dominican monk appears astonished as the visitor continues.

> Shouldn't you just have hay for sleeping? Also, the pictures on the
> wall in my room Of the Virgin Mary and the cross, surely it isn't
> necessary for you people to remind yourselves what you should
> be contemplating. I would think the images in your mind would
> suffice.

MONK

Yes, yes. I think you are correct.

His eyes narrow. The visitor could tell that the monk would give his ideas some thought.

KONRAD

I must confess, last night I felt something was missing, some mystical quality is absent from these hallowed grounds. It strikes me that there are no Gregorian chants being sung. I must say I am disappointed in not seeing you and the other monks walking together in the courtyard garden and halls in the late evening, singing in the candlelight. Is this not part of . . .

FO

...Konrad's mind goes into focus and he hears the word Catholicism and agnostic Buddhist, laughter . . . and then his mind fades away again ...

FI

MONK

Well, I'm afraid times, they have changed, no?

The padre is a bit embarrassed.

VISITOR

Do you not tremble, even a little, Father, when you realize that if God has an ear with which to hear, there will be little to listen to?"

MONK

Indeed sir, I understand what you are saying, but our time is taken in so many ways. The business of managing this establishment with all of its extra facilities for social endeavors and...

The Padre stops abruptly, realizing the nature of what he had just said.

[Several days later]

The visitor prepares to leave. It is that evening after a meal that Father Martina once again approaches the visitor who is finishing his wine.

> MONK
>
> You have me thinking a little. I'm worried that we, the monastics, may be on a wayward path that is not fulfilling our duties in many ways.

The visitor studies the father's face and speaks.

> VISITOR
>
> Father, I have just finished reading Eugene O'Neill's play Mourning Becomes Electra. The hate, violence, and treachery of the human mind brought forth in this play convinces me that you have been on the right path for centuries, and that there shall always be a necessity for a monk and his thoughts.

A jolly expression returns to the father's face. They both shake hands and the visitor reaches down for his luggage, standing in the doorway. Father Martina is first to speak.

> MONK
>
> Must you leave so soon? Your stay has been an interesting one for me. We shall miss you.

> VISITOR
>
> Thank you, but I have to be on my way. Good-bye, Father.

Startled, Father Martina turns.

Oh, Father Superior, I did not see you standing there. Who was that man you ask? He was an atheist—just passing through.

FO

FI

39. Ext/Yacht—Night

[Scene]

Konrad realizes the guests are leaving, and finds himself in the parking area of the wharf beside Adele. She lights a cigarette and places her hand upon his knee. Konrad feels drunk. He holds Adele close to him and caresses her deeply.

[The next morning]

40. INT/HOTEL—DAY

He awakens in the hotel room. The phone is ringing.

41. INT/TRAIN—DAY.

He awakens again and finds himself on the train. He cautiously asks the man sitting next to him the destination of the train—much to the surprise of the older gentleman.

OLDER GENTLEMAN

"San Francisco."

KONRAD (to himself)

Was I to meet Adele in San Fran? No. Why am I going to San Francisco? Adele, I can see her now, sitting across the table in a restaurant. But I can't remember if it happened or do I just think it happened?

Konrad fights off his wandering mind. He must get off. He must return to San Diego. He must. He must write....

VO

42. EXT/RIVER BANK—DAY

KONRAD (to himself)

Piles of rusty cans mixed with generous portions of jagged bottles with mud-splattered labels, half filled with rain water and heaped upon more and more junk forming complex lines and shades of light and dark as if it were a sepia sketch. Within the boundaries lay an assemblage of forgotten things, yet somehow the junkyard by the river still possesses a certain dignity, for it is also the home of an old hermit. The winter had been long and cold, but the old man survived another one and this was the first warm sunny day forecasting Spring. The old man came out of his tin hut like a bear out of hibernation and after an appropriate amount of stretching, sat on his favorite metal oil drum not far from the door and began the important task of whittling on a stick.

HERMIT

The sun feels real good.

The sun had always been important to him. He begins reminiscing of his boyhood days on a small farm . . . lying on the porch of the old country house... the late morning sun gently warming his face . . . out in the yard, the rope swing hanging from a large juniper tree ... a pigeon flapping abruptly from beneath the eves . . . hearing Grandma in the kitchen and Uncle Owen at the well . . .a slight breeze clattering the cottonwood leaves. This was his life many years ago and such remembrances were worth more than gold to him.

Today will be different. Reaching an old can, He pulls out a hook. Two weeks ago the river had dropped enough to fish. Fresh mud stands thick below the doorstep of the shack. Looking up into the hot sun, the old man, his chin and throat covered with white stubble, mumbles to himself.

I'm gonna get a big catfish today.

At noon, the riverbanks are coated with steaming mud. Just below the shack, patches of long grass are matted together, recently flattened by the high waters. The center of the river is still dangerously turbulent. Limbs and trash float not far from the edge. Piles of driftwood accumulate down the river. It is here, down river that the old man decides to try his luck. His stiff and calloused fingers fumble in the coffee can full of rusty hooks, until he finds the right one.

This ought to do it.

A look of optimism spreads over his face. He stands up at the doorway of the one-room hut. The sun burns his balding head and shines only a few inches into the doorway of the shanty's dark interior. Inside is an iron bed and a wooden table standing with a shelf above it. Cardboard patchwork helps line one wall where empty cans are piled. The old man carries his pole and a can of worms down to the river's edge over newly lain planks.

He has risen before daylight to light the camp stove and brew coffee so that he can carry the heavy boards from the stack behind the shanty and put them over the soft mud before sunrise.

Now he is able to get to the river punt that waits patiently, while being slapped on its bottom by the shallow waves. He is proud of the boat he had made four summers ago and, although it leaks now and then, it serves him well. He will test it again today in the still churning waters of the river. The old man pats the boat like it is a faithful horse as he climbs into it. Shielding his eyes from the bright sun with his hand, he gazes out at the swirls of muddy water. Having lived with the river, he knows it is still too early to challenge its treachery. He and the river have fought for many years now and he had come close to drowning several times. For many weeks the flood has kept him inside, but he has to fish today. After dragging the makeshift anchor, a frayed rope with a rock tied to the end, he picks up a paddle and sticks it into the mud.

The boat does not budge. He curses the mud and tries the other side. Slowly the punt moves into the swift current near the shore and he is able to paddle, only to steer towards a huge pile of limbs and sticks. Coming alongside a overhanging limb, he puts the paddles in the boat and grabs the limb and pulls himself underneath. The smell of soggy wood and warm mud fills the air. The sun bares down and soon the cork begins to bob. The old man looks to one side, as if he were uninterested, like a cat when it sees a mouse. The cork disappears and the line draws taut.

It's a fair-sized one.

He pulls back, feeling the vibration that is so peculiar to a line cutting crosswise through theeddies. The tension on the cord disappears. The old man realizes the fish line is snagged in the debris and branches below. Then he smells something besides the hot mud. Smoke! Looking upstream, he sees smoke curling from the shack. He props the pole in the water, grabs a paddle, pushes on the pile and then reaches for the other paddle. His head hits a large limb overhead.

Opening his eyes, he is blinded by the sun and finds himself lying in the bottom of the boat. He pulls himself up, but feels dizzy and sick as he squints, looking at the shack again. Flames are flickering along the edges of the roof. The boat is still stuck against the pile of debris. After freeing it, he rows hard, fighting the strong currents and finally brings the boat along the river's edge to the shack. The punt hits the bank and he throws the rock anchor into the mud. He then puts the paddles out onto the bank and leaps onto them. Several days later, some people discover a dead old man half buried, near the smoldering remains of a shack. In the center of the mighty river, the water is still treacherously turbulent....

43. EXT/TRAIN STATION—DAY

Finally Konrad manages to get off the train, which stops at a small town not far from San Fran. After getting his ticket for the next train back to San Diego, he walks over onto the platform and stares at the empty tracks below him...

VO

KONRAD (To himself)

Konstas watches a sparrow on the track for a moment and then turns to Makis,

KONSTAS

The train is late today.

It Is Makis who brakes a long period of silence.

MAKIS

It's a shame.

KONSTAS

Yes, indeed, it's downright tragic. And he was good crossing guard too.

MAKIS

Yes, yes he was, reliable too.

KONSTAS

Who do you think they'll get to replace him? Maybe Andrea?

MAKIS

Don't know, I have no idea. No idea. Where did you say they were taking him, Konstas?

KONSTAS

To some mental hospital outside Thessaloniki. I couldn't believe how a man could go down hill so fast. It all started with that letter from the head station master just two months ago. Niko showed it to me himself. He was heartbroken. That vine meant the world to him. It was all he had left after his wife, daughter, and uncle were executed during the war. So the vine was a bit scraggly looking. It's as Niko said, it had been his closest friend for these past years after the war. Remember I gave him some excuse that day so as to leave earlier than usual. You know he and I used to talk for hours about our adventurous escapades in the resistance. But, just think, the real breaking point was when they came to dig up that old vine. It was all over then—just as if a Nazi bullet struck him in the temple.

FO

FI

44. EXT/BUS STATION—DAY

[Scene]

Carlotta finds Konrad wandering about the bus station that is only five blocks from the house. As she takes his hand, he begins talking to her as if she had been beside him all day.

FI

FO

KONRAD (to himself)

. . . I'll always remember Dublin in the fall. I enrolled at the University of Dublin to study early Irish history and was searching for a room. I rang the bell and since there was no answer, I went around to the side of this old two-story house and I knocked at the screen door. Footsteps . . . door was sticking . . . opened . . . I was in shock ... it was Ann, the Ann that I had written about all these years. I could only stare as she asked if I had come about the room. I climbed the stairs to the landing and was confronted by a sunny porch like room extending across the frontage of the house.

I said it was very nice and tried desperately to keep my eyes from searching her face. I was somewhat taken aback to learn that the rope and sheets were a divide—my side versus hers. I'm not a prude, but since it was Ann, I would have taken it no matter what the arrangement. The weeks went by and Ann and I would take walks in a nearby wooded section on the outskirts of the city. On a late October day, the leaves were already becoming brownish but neither of us really paid much attention—we kicked our way through them, giggling like high school kids.

And then it happened—we both went down frolicking and we kissed. Nothing was said—it had been so natural but yet everything we did for the rest of that sunny afternoon was so different—so meaningful and every now and then we caught each other staring into each other's eyes, yet not searchingly—just to be looking—just to be enjoying each other.

The crisp blue sky had that chill in the air. Such weather always reminded me of football and graduate school days at the University of Missouri. It was later that evening that something very strange happened. I was holding her and we were both gazing out at a treetop level from an opened apartment window. The sun had set and the evening sounds drifted through the neighborhood— sounds of children playing down the street. A certain quietness suddenly came over everything. Ann turned her face up to mine and whispered somewhat frightened . . . "What is it?" I replied that it is a magic moment . . . one of the rarest things that can happen. We both sat silently awestruck as I held her tenderly and the moment slowly faded....

FO

45. INT/HOUSE—DAY

[Scene]

The next day Konrad returns to the Ensenada hotel. He begins to write another love letter to Ann in the Hummingbird plot.

FO

KONRAD (typing)

Dear Ann,

I love you. Now what? I look upon these few days with you as some of the happiest and saddest moments in my life. I wouldn't trade them for anything. Remember kindly of me, for all my lies were meant to be able to bring happiness to you ultimately. I'm reading Cannery Row now. It's a poem, a stink, a grating noise, a quality light, a tone, a habit, a nostalgia, a dream . . . and it could be the most beautiful place in the world . . . I think this may describe our relationship.

Love, Howard

Konrad yells for Carlotta and then apologizes.

46.EXT/HOUSE—DAY

KONRAD

I'm sorry, I feel depressed because I was just fired from my San Fran Herald job for being anti-nationalistic.

Carlotta looks sympathetic.

CARLOTTA (to herself)

He has indeed been fired, but it was several months ago. I understand English fairly well but he rambles too fast for me.

KONRAD

So my views on international law are somewhat idealistic—that all political borders should be dissolved and all passports destroyed. Only local areas of governing, albeit from a variety of viewpoints, would allow people to choose which they believed were best. Yet all local and regional governing bodies would be coordinated through a United Nations-type central government. This would allow people who were starving at any one place on the globe to move to where food could be obtained or at least grown or developed. Thousands of years later, one race with one language would evolve and there would be no more wars.

Carlotta sits attentively, understanding little.

I must go for a run now.

Konrad takes off down towards the beach in the noonday sun after he drinks a large mug of rum.

CARLOTTA (to herself)

I see him in the moonlight running in and out of the surf like a sandpiper just staying out of the reach of the foaming surf.

[Days pass]

The Hummingbird novel thickens proportional to the running. Konrad writes the running chapters quickly, but finds himself wanting to emulate Howard....

Howard becomes a fantastic runner, which even causes a breakup with his wife. He begins to run competitively in many road races . . . running, running, run, run—pushing ahead, driving action of the arms, wind passing over ears, blasting, forcing air out and then expanding the chest with great sucking of air, exhilarating effort, the sensation of speed, the passing scenery, the churning power up the steep hill, the incredible peacefulness of cruising effortlessly downhill, sweat, cooling, mile after mile, pounding the pavement, vibration of solid thighs, free, wild, striving, competitive, straining against time, to conquer and overcome, to extend oneself to the limit, to strive against forces with the individual self-force, flowing with rhythm, the poetry of motion, the beauty of body movement, fatigue, to pass the mark, to have participated and finally the contentment of fulfillment and achievement.

Howard enters a marathon in the preceding chapter and so Konrad, confused and feeling jealous of Howard's prowess in the presence of Ann, enters the ten kilometer road race in San Diego, returning physically and mentally exhausted. He begins writing fanatically, striving in desperation to reach Ann...

FI

46. EXT/HOTEL PATIO—DAY

KONRAD (to himself)

For over a year I have waited for this moment. I know she will leave her room as soon as I begin to play the piano. Her room overlooks the plaza with its small bridge. My ground-level balcony faces the direction of her room. The light of dusk filters through the palms outside my window as I begin to play, strong melodic, then soft, romantic. The sounds lift to her opened veranda. I know she must be hearing familiar music at this moment.

My trembling execution of the next few bars disappears as I think of the gentle, lovely woman across the way. She would remember, she must. As the slow passages proceed, I stare at the dark doorway behind her balcony across the plaza of this little village of Mallorca. She had come here several years ago to escape from the tragic night of her performance in which she faltered and destroyed the presentation.

Soon after, she had given up—given up life and music. A great pianist at twenty, now a withdrawn soul, torturing herself over the past. But now I have found her . . . she is coming to the balcony . . . she is near. The decrescendo section continues. The tempo increases—allegro molto appassionato, then subsides. Next a large crescendo, strong, vibrant, giving her strength, a strength to come forward out into the world again—to life to play her music once more. I know it's all within her. She is gone again, but hopefully will reappear below.

I can see whitecaps beginning to form on the sea near the cliffs to the south. The sunset's orange blaze strikes the glass pane of my veranda door. I play on and there, across the plaza, standing statuesque in a lovely, white flowing dress, is the creature of all love, all essence of woman, all beauty, all meaning to my life. She steps forward and I play on and on, fanatically, prestissimo, followed by rolling passage after passage—ritardondo.

Oh, how I hope. All these years of yearning, I pray. She is walking slowly, mesmerized by the music—her music. No one else could know. She is walking over the small walkway bridge. My tears blur the keyboard. The notes come fast, the chords enlarge, allegro con brio, then a moment of stillness, a few tender notes, pianissimo. Her concerto is coming to an end. She sees me at the piano. She knows who I am. She realized why I am playing with all my heart. She is running. There in full view, she stands before me. I finish. Her face beaming among her tears—Ann whispers, Konrad, Oh Konrad.

FO

FI

47. EXT/HOUSE—DAY

KONRAD (to himself)

My legs still ache from the pounding they received in the San Diego race, but I will continue to type. I will now write Ann a letter. No Howard must write Ann...

[Two months later]

Konrad meets and stays with Adele. Never does the situation go very smoothly. There is an argument about the economic philosophy of Hegel. Neither are adamant. Adele becomes infatuated with Konrad and Konrad finds Adele intellectually stimulating after spending many "silent" hours with Carlotta. One afternoon while window shopping with Adele, Konrad follows Adele to her apartment and they have lunch together. Adele looks deep into Konrad's face.

KONRAD

What's the matter?

ADELE

I'm simply trying to understand you.

She would challenge him.

What about the concept of the individual? If a Siamese twin can be connected at the level of the brain, then in principle, there could be a series of such individuals with such "duo-brains" connected say with visual pathways to two sets of eyes so that each set of eyes simultaneously read different political ideologies. What do you think would be come of that person, Konrad?

KONRAD

Such a mind could only be conjectured. It would depend upon the extent and level of connection of the duo-brains and thereby the definition of an individual mind. One could extend the concept of connected brains in series. Then what would be the individual mind—the composite series?

ADELE (to herself)

I'm impressed. He has not only answered intelligently, but has expanded on the concept and I attended a scientific debate on the subject just a month ago and nobody had thought of that idea.

ADELE

But Konrad, what is the individual mind—a pattern of engrams on two cerebral hemispheres of a brain?

KONRAD

I don't think so.

KONRAD (to himself)

Now I'll play chess with this gal.

KONRAD

If a person loses a leg—he still is an individual. To what extent can the individual lose of itself and still be an individual to exist since brain function must be a biological gradient?

KONRAD (to himself)

I've not yet checkmated her, but close to it.

KONRAD

One would like a strict operational concept for a definition of the term individual and best suited for such a purpose for humans seems to be the mind.

KONRAD (to himself)

I've slipped out of her trap.

ADELE

If the brain waves of one area of a brain that has been cultured in a vessel, like that one in the novel Donovan's Brain by that writer, oh, who was it?

KONRAD

Sidomak.

KONRAD (to himself)

I've scored.

ADELE

As I was saying, if these waves are produced, to what extent must the gradient of engrams patterns be in order to say that the individual's mind exists?

KONRAD

Let me see, you're asking quantitatively to what extent and qualitatively which areas of the brain are required before the individual exists? Right?

KONRAD (to himself)

I'm being pushed again.

ADELE

Or visa versa. How little functional mind must there be before it is said to be cognitive and existent and thereby signifying an individual?

KONRAD (to himself)

I've had enough of this play.

KONRAD

One could visualize that neural nets might function between fused cat and human frontal lobe regions such that one might have catlike interpretations of human initiated thought. What is the meaning of 'I'? One operational definition would be that it is a particular array of engram patterns that is cognizant of its existence. But the I or individual may be based upon a non-typical engram pattern such as a cat/human mosaic, etc. Also, with the advent of artificial intelligence, even these concepts have to be extended. Conceivably, there might be biomechanical connections of biological minds with artificial ones at an electronic level.

ADELE

I have something to do in the kitchen.

47. INT/ADELE'S APARTMENT—NIGHT

That night Konrad continues to write letters to Ann in the Hummingbird novel; many times confusing Howard's signature with his own. In fact the novel's plot has turned into an obsession of pure letter writings and his affair with love for Ann intensified....

V.O.

KONRAD (typing)

Dear Ann,

I'm now in the student's room on the Cave Hill Campus with sea air blowing quietly across me through the slotted windows. My business here went like a machine. The Writer's Guild of the Caribbean is impressed with my writings, but I am only impressed with how much poetry is in a person. The poetry of you is just now beginning to take its toll. I'm going mad actually. I went to the beach searching for something—anything. I sought eagerly the face of the others. Somewhere here you have to be in their midst. Somewhere you have to be within touching distance. Somewhere, I began to choke, the tears are now finally beginning to stream, it hurts. How long will it hurt?

Love, Howard

Adele and Konrad leave a restaurant when she notices that Konrad is in a dazed state. She decides to take him to her apartment and after a cooling drink she put him to bed. Moments later she is lying close to his somewhat feverish body. In the morning, Adele is surprised to hear her typewriter and turns to find Konrad up. She slips on a robe and walks into the living room to find Konrad typing frantically . . .

KONRAD (typing)

Howard meets Kim, a world class ultra-marathoner, during the Stockholm marathon. She befriends Howard and teaches him the ins and outs of ultra-marathon running. Howard thinks of Ann and begins a letter after his race in Barbados . . . Konrad is still feverish and continues to type madly. Adele slowly moves behind Konrad and begins reading the typed pages beside the typewriter. Konrad does not even notice her as he continues....

Dear Ann,

A piña colada, please. I will drink deeply to again taste the incredible excitement that I had known with you, but to no avail. The tears are streaming down my cheeks as I write. It is not the same. It will never be the same. We who have held hands on a dark road. We who had laughed ridiculous laughs, laughing at nothing. We who have loved the warmth of each others company and shared the emotions of a Caribbean night. We were lovers yet was that the meaning, can that be the meaning?

I truly believe that it will take a lifetime or two to tire of such feelings. I will always be searching for your smile, the charm of one person, incredible that I will look searchingly into other faces to see if that same something can be found. How ridiculous, yet I search, trying to keep my sanity, fooling myself into thinking that maybe in this one's face the quality of that endearing look of kindness, that rare once in the world of time, could there possibly be there in front of me the same.

How frail time is, how fleeting the precious moments, the tears continue to stream. How long can they stream? How much of you is now me? How much of me is now you? Can time destroy? Then let the test begin. Nothing, not distance, not the lack of seeing those dark brown eyes—yet these little things are accumulating, building. I now know that nothing can destroy my love for you, that nothing can destroy the images of you. I now understand universality, the passion that extends beyond passion, the soul of you, the beauty of you, the goodness of you, you are heaven and earth. Now there will be no schedules, no daily routines, now that I have found you, I will lightly pass through days that in turn will grow into continuums of yes's and no's—words only vaguely to be heard and recognized . . .

Love, Konrad

Adele is fascinated with Konrad's flow of words and asks him why he signed it "Konrad." He has not been fully aware of Adele's presence beside him and is momentarily startled, then confused, but finally realizes the mistaken signature. Konrad continues to meet Adele at luncheons at a particular hotel. As he waits in the hotel lobby he jots down notes for further development of the Hummingbird plot . . . Ann tells Jack she must help a very dear friend . . . Jack is her business partner that she lives with . . . Jack guesses she has a great deal of past love for Howard, but when she tells me that she is going to see her father in Great Falls and adds that she will be back, he answers—of course you will. Why wouldn't you? Ann then catches an Eastern Airlines plane to New Jersey, where the run is in progress, to meet Howard.

KONRAD (to himself)

Dear Ann,

I run in the sand, the waves hit, the cross-wave, the foam, the same foam that I have seen pass over our feet, but it is different foam, it is terribly different foam, it is just foam. Three blacks walk by. What are they thinking? What are they saying? I would not have understood had they spoken to me.

I am in a world of love, a million or so light years away from them. They are in the world of reality. At last, something to bring me to this world—a beautiful torso, a blond, but so what, it doesn't have any meaning. A myriad of torsos couldn't be equivalent to even one of your smiles. I am screaming inside, I am going mad, I know it now, how can I stand it that someone, anyone, can be enjoying your smile, which I would easily pay at least a million torsos for and that person would not even realize he was getting a million-torso smile.

Oh my God, my God, even I didn't realize what those smiles really meant to me, even I have wasted them. Oh, forgive me, what precious moments, what total madness of me not to somehow

221

convey what those smiles mean—not now to be able to reach out and touch your lips, your hair, now that you're away from me....

Love, Konrad

FI

48. INT/AIRPORT—DAY

Konrad and Adele are waiting in the San Fran airport for the plane with Murray to arrive from Seattle. The conversation turns to its usual intellectual arguments involving some topics as Shostakovich concertos and the French contemporary artist Vlaminck to the mechanistic derivation of pain and death. Konrad notices that there are several people walking towards him but they seem different somehow.

KONRAD (to himself)

They are slightly unreal. Why am I feeling afraid of them or am I? As I look around the mall, the whole place seems strange, as if . . . I am confused . . . what am I? This is something or nothing . . . what was happening?

What should I do? I will try to control myself, although I feel that I have no control over the situation. I will walk in with very little confidence towards that bench in the middle of the mall. If I can just make it to that bench.

Now I will sit down. Things are not right. People are not the way they should be somehow, as if from some other place. They are acting slightly different and their clothes are not quite the usual. I cannot see Adele. I am beginning to panic, but I do not dare attempt to get up from the bench. I think I see her walking out through the main door. She is probably looking for me, so I'll force myself to my feet and dart through the door.

Catching her by the shoulder, she turns. It is not Adele and she begins speaking in Portuguese. Konrad apologizes and she answers in English without the slightest hint of an accent. He dashes back to the doors. They are push-type doors.

KONRAD (to himself)

But I could have sworn they were, moments before, sliding doors.

Festive music comes from the street, as a group in papier-mâché caricature costumes are dancing all over the street. At that moment, Konrad notices a sign above in Portuguese and the buildings appear different. He turns and goes quickly back through the sliding doors into the mall.

KONRAD (to himself)

The bench is still there and . . . and sliding doors, yes they were sliding doors that I had opened. The parade is gone.

ADELE

Konrad

KONRAD (to himself)

I glance behind me and see her coming toward me but, what seems to be in slow motion. Her voice and image is fading as she comes closer to me. Spider-like images begin creeping across the virtually frozen view before me as Adele, with infinite slowness, comes toward me. A multitude of different noises begin to get louder and louder. The spiderlike branches become voices and the view changes before me once again. I find myself gazing out from a window of a hotel room down onto a street.

Before me, people are hurrying busily below. A streetcar is clanging its bell and moves along a midway beneath the spidery trees. There are posters in Portuguese on the side of the tram. I hear my name once more and then I see Adele. She is asking me if I feel alright. I continue to sit on the bench in the hall and make some attempt at being composed.

ADELE

Murray will be arriving at Gate 23, they said. Shall we go down, Konrad?

FI

[Later]

49. INT/BUS—DAY

Konrad reminisces over his conversation with Adele while on the bus back to Ensenada.

KONRAD (to himself)

I said good-bye, telling her that I did not want to give up Carlotta, and that I didn't love her for now I realize that I am confusing her for Ann. Adele cries and says that I didn't mean these things, that I am sick and that I am only trying not to hurt her because I am afraid I may become very ill and that I will need someone like Carlotta simply to take care of me. I don't know. Maybe she's right.

50. INT/HOTEL—DAY

As soon as Konrad arrives at the Ensenada hotel Konrad's mind quickly shifts to his obsession of writing letters to Ann...

VO

51. EXT/BEACH—DAY

KONRAD (narrates)

Dear Ann,

I hear myself breathe as I lie on my back in the gentle water. Dusk begins. My chest moves. Air comes swiftly rising in, rumbling out again. The waves lap at my ears with hollow sounds. I open my eyes. The sun settles over Barbados. The tears continue, in my mind they will continue to stream until perhaps we meet when once again I will search through some crowd and there standing before me, will be the greatest goddess of all historical time, you, and those standing about will not even be aware of it.

52. INT/BAR—DAY

KONRAD (to himself)

Can't they see? Can't they understand what that radiance is and where it is coming from? Time for one more drink. I look at the bartender.

KONRAD

One more drink.

That part is said, is heard.

KONRAD (to himself)

What isn't heard is the rest of my conversation to him. Can't he tell? Can't he understand what I am quietly screaming to him— that I'm in love! In love with a beautiful woman. I'm in love?

Can't you hear me?

KONRAD (to himself)

I will continue to work and I will continue to drink. The rotating fan above me, slowly revolves, generating shadows, shadows of despair, shadows of unending monotony with incessant streaming of tears—oh those tears. Why must they continue? What anguish, yet somehow sadly beautiful. I shall never forget you, and furthermore I refuse to even let you out of my mind. Our lives have passed somewhat, but possibly by some strange quirk, it has just begun . . . God take precious care of you for I trust no one else for the job.

Love, Konrad

FI

53. EXT/KONRAD'S VERANDA—NIGHT

The evening turns to night. Carlotta sits beside Konrad on the veranda and looks at the stars hanging in the moonless skies.

CARLOTTA (to herself)

Who or where was he now?

Konrad is in the stars. Konrad places his hand over hers.

KONRAD (to himself)

I remember riding the transcontinental across Canada when I was in my youth.

[Scene]

Two birds wings fast, cutting thru crosswinds
Low passing clouds sweep by

Over shower-swept land below appears
Morning light breaking through the sky
The train sped past shadows on the ground
Amid a bright full moon
For now behind is Winnipeg
And beyond is Saskatoon
Telephone lines and telephone poles
Reaching across yellow fields flat
Furrows and fences at edges rushing
The horizon extending itself, and yet
Just ahead a little further, further on and further
Continuing on and on and on and on and on and on...

KONRAD

You know Carlotta, I used to live in a little village in Maine by the coast. It was a little cove. I had an old wooden sloop—a twenty-foot knockabout with full keel. I gaff rigged her and after scraping her down, I repainted her topside black and her keel with copper bottom paint. I gave her a name, I think it was the Suzy-Lynn or was it the Shark?

[Scene]

Anyway, I sailed her proudly in the Gulls Cove. The brown canvas sails and the short bowsprit suited her. Sure she leaked, but I bailed her bilge like pampering a mistress. She was the best looking boat in the rocky ledged cove.

Several weeks before, I ran her down the rails from dry dock and she took afloat at high tide. I had fitted her with all the fineries I could afford—shiny brass chocks, brass fairleads, brass gudgeon and pintle and copper cleats. She had become a very close friend. The waves lapped at her sides and she dipped her port waterway flirtatiously at me—inviting me to join her for a sail. . . .

. . . Watch out! The boom is caught in the mainsheet. The mainsail is straining against what must be a gusty thirty-knot wind. If

227

I let go of the rope, she'll likely broach. But I can't hang on much longer to both the rudder and main-sheet. There she goes! A complete yaw, boom broad off. Hull broad to the wind. She's heeling hard. I've got to bring her into the wind...

54. EXT/HOUSE—NIGHT

CARLOTTA

Konrad. Konrad . . . you're here, you're okay.

Carlotta holds him tightly. He looks into her face and then cries a moment.

KONRAD

What is it? I don't really know. There are all these past sights that keep appearing to me. Maybe if I write they will go away.

55. INT/KITCHEN—NIGHT

Konrad goes into the kitchenette area and retrieves the typewriter from the bedroom floor.... Konrad begins typing.

Mist drips from each pine needle
Onto entangled wild rose below
Seared from weeks of drought and sun
Brown oat-grass, now soaked and heavy
Bends over thirsty cornflowers
A light breeze sways young honey locust
And vireo flicker among the saplings
Fog sifts through high lodge-pole pine
As washing sounds of waves on shore
Echo against a rock ledge beyond
Light becomes less and grey becomes
greyer
My day is rapidly dying

Konrad shuts off the light and returns out onto the veranda with Carlotta.

56. EXT/VERANDA—NIGHT

KONRAD

You understand if I told you I don't pray, it's not so much disrespect, its more from confusion. If I were to pray, it would be to thank God for the opportunity to be an introspective being, you know, one that knows that it exists and what the chances were that it would never exist in the first place.

I danced among the stars for but a moment of eternity and, although I was awed, I was also disdainful of the suffering that occurred about me. You see, Carlotta, the meaning of existence appears to be as follows . . .When muscle comes to be—it contracts and does work. When the brain comes to be, it thinks and strives to understand.

Mystical extensions of trying to understand seem reasonable—to worship a creator and give thanks for your existence seems correct. But why create worshiping entities in the first place? -- Especially amid so much grief and imperfection. Then there is the mystery of the individual.

What is the individual? What am I? An aggregate of atoms in a particular pattern at a particular time, soon to be redistributed for other things? Of course, my existence wasn't too difficult before I was born.

EXT/HOUSE-NIGHT

CARLOTTA (to herself in Spanish)

I believe that, that I am understanding, for the first time, Konrad's ramblings in English. I will sleep under the stars tonight for somehow they seemed more like friends . . . and I will speak to them in Spanish . . .

I have gazed in awe at your home—a study in masterful creation—the vast heavens and humbly bow my head before your Omni-power, for I understand but little and believe in faith too much since I have looked upon you and talked with you day by day as a person not stopping to realize my centricity in doing such. I, if even one may speak of this with any fact except faith, again wish to express my gratefulness whatever your meanings may be my appreciation for my existence in reality and may I place a stamp of prayer along with this letter, saying that hope is in my heart that you also have an ear to hear my wish.

FI

57. INT/HOUSE—DAY

[Scene]

Carlotta rolls over, opens her eyes slowly and sees Konrad between the openings of the brick lattice. He too has slept near the veranda to catch some of the cooling night breezes. She hears Konrad mumbling to himself.

KONRAD

I feel like Johann Bolyai the great mathematician when he wrote his father. 'I have created a new universe from nothing.'

[Scene]

Konrad stands looking directly into the sun. His nostrils flare.

Carlotta does not understand what he is saying. She goes to the kitchen area and pours herself a cool glass of mango juice and sits down on the makeshift bedding behind the lattice wall. She begins to worry about Konrad being in the sun so long. A pair of black-throated green warblers and a yellow throated viero sing a non-rehearsed contrapuntal chorus in the swaying jacaranda branches. Konrad hears no songs.

Konrad begins walking back and forth, agitated and sweating profusely. Something must be wrong. Something that started this must have goofed. Who started this? God? God. Who is God? Who gave God power to do this or even the idea of reality, or are there other realities, or real-like systems, better or worse than this one. What about beauty? What is beautiful? A beautiful deer is one that has healthy fur and bright clear eyes. But beauty is complicated. For example, a Leonardo da Vinci drawing of an ugly old man who reflects sickness, old age and strife.

So what might be considered a beautiful drawing or may be either a perfect crystal or a rare stone or a sepia sketch of a messy dump with all its connotations of rotten smells. I doubt that the universe was made for beauty per se. Beauty is a response of complicated receptor-minded systems as a pleasurable experience—nothing more.

60. EXT/HOUSE—DAY

Then Konrad blurts out,

KONRAD

I hate you! I hate you!

He is now in a rage. He begins shaking his fist at the sky and cursing God.

I'm striving to understand what the meaning of it all is, but you won't help me understand.

Konrad is in mental agony.

You tell me—do you hear.

Konrad collapses to the deck floor. Carlotta rushes out to him.

[Scene]

Below the smashing waves tear at the lava breccias and crash into the caves that are producing thundering sounds.

[Later that evening]

There is a cool stillness as Konrad awakes to the smell of roasting guachinango fish. Carlotta has also prepared some cactus tunas that she and Konrad begin eating with the fish, along with some mild cheese, and white rum A rare moment of peace comes to Konrad and soon Carlotta realizes he no longer is listening to her. At last Konrad's mind turns off. But he feels a great surge of melancholia as if he would not be able to handle it. His mind swirls and he grabs at the typewriter directly before him, so as not to fall from his chair. It is his mind that is turning and turning . . . he must write, write, write....

[Scene]

HERNANDO

The cheese, it is good, no?

He nibbles at the cheese and then drinks quickly of the tequila. His whiskers twist as he speaks. Hernando's ears are tiny and tight against his head. His beady eyes become bright when he learns of Jose's new conquest. He continues to push food into his stomach as he listens to Jose and of the woman of the "barrios de bajo." Solidad is a woman and men understand what that means. They grab her "behind" as she passes them. She snaps back at them. She works at the bar on the street next to the casucha houses. Her hips sway sensually. The soles of her sandals are made of used tires. The right one is the most worn because of a limp—Solidad's only imperfection.

The men never tease her about it. Her limp is unimportant to them. They respect her sexy ways too much. She is like a cat at night when the lights and shadows of the street appear. The people become different and they move more slowly. She is able to prowl. The night will be hot.

[Scene]

61. INT/APARTMENT—NIGHT

Hernando has managed to lure Solidad to his apartment. He gives her much food. His feet begin to paw at her pelvis under the table. Soon he is dragging his stolen necklace across her breasts. She moves with excitement. He has his fill of her and rolls her away from his fat stomach, still breathing heavily.

KONRAR (narrates)

Ernie is next to get Solidad. He promises to take her to Las Vegas, to the bright lights and slot machines. They make it to the outskirts of a Harlingen motel where he rapes her. Ernie drives off in his flashy yellow Chevrolet. Solidad hitch-hikes back across the river bridge. Lately Solidad has been feeling sad and alone with everyone and everything.

SOLIDAD

Why must I strive? Why do I think of God? The mind is playing tricks on me. My mind must exist because I have a thoughts. Before I existed I was nothing. After I exist am I nothing? I am confused. What should I do? What should I not do?

Solidad likes Jose. He is good looking.

62.EXT/CITY PARK—NIGHT

Solidad and Jose stand together. Jose takes Solidad's hand and presses it to his body. The night breeze move the palm leaves above them. She bites his lip. He bites her neck. They drop to the ground. Both moan loudly. The pink light in the sky has gone.

[Months later]

Solidad's belly begins to grow. She does not want Jose's child. The men of the barrios pay little notice to her change. One night she sends a small boy to get a doctor. He has been drinking but is able to help Solidad. The premature baby is not right from the beginning. Solidad buys tortillas at the store not far from the bar for sixteen pesos. With them she stops her hunger. Her milk is not good. The baby boy does not grow and soon becomes sick.

One day Solidad takes it to the Clinica de Federal. She stands in line for many hours that morning but returns without having seen the doctor. The baby cries weakly throughout the night. At dawn a chicken crows. The baby no longer cries. Solidad puts the dead baby into a plastic bag and slips outside. She places the bag into a large trash can.

Solidad never attends mass. She does not have a nice dress. She steps into the doorway to gaze into the cathedral. She gives a little prayer for the baby boy in the trash. Solidad has pains in her stomach. They finally go away but during the last few days she begins to cough. The night of a big rain, two boys push their way into her shack. They have fun with her. She was too weak to care. Her fever makes her hear Jose's voice. The boys leave her on the floor. She opens the door and walks into the cooling rain.

Soon she comes to the preacher's hut. She goes inside. It is warm. The hand of the preacher touches her thigh. He has drunk much rum during the storm. The flames from the stove flicker on her face. She yearns for Jose as the scaly hand passes up her dress. She screams,

SOLIDAD

No!

She pushes him against the hot stove. She runs from the hut into the rain. The sewers have backed up. Several dead rats float by. She stumbles. She feels cold and sick. She is tired of running from men. She places her face into the running water of the gutter. She hears less and less of the rain on the tin roof beside her.

Konrad stops typing again—

A pajaro-fragta [frigate bird] sweeps over the rocks below. Birds, birds . . . birds!

KONRAD (typing)

To Kill a Chickadee . . .

His fingers pass over the keys frantically.

>Listen well to the chirping
>And the songs from Meadow Sparrows
>They may be telling the secrets of life forces.
>Our lives of work and strife are reflected
>By our feather friends
>Soaring above us all the time
>All beginnings and all ends

Noon and minus twenty below... I venture into the unknown of the back orchard wading knee deep in the frosted snow, Crystals upon crystals. I always wished to be among the stars and here I am amidst millions of little stars. Blinking bedazzling me from the blinding sun's reflection off the crusted surface.

I struggle in deep snow, overhead frozen frosted branches, before me a robin! Resting apparently quite comfortably, basking in each morsel of heat, obtainable from the bright sun. It looks at me as curiously as I look at it. But why is the robin here? January seventeenth and minus twenty degrees. A robin before me as if to purposefully perplex. To warn me of something perhaps, but what?

DRAFT BOARD OFFICIAL

> Next man. Let me introduce myself. I am a member of your neighborhood draft board. Have you ever killed? Could you kill if it were necessary? Do you have anything against killing? For instance, some religious belief. Or let me put it this way. You might have killed a bird when you were driving over here. So you may have already killed. Sign here.

[Scene]

The faint light of late evening meets the deepening mysteries of night. My young arms barely reach the asphalt overhang of our garage. Scampering to the roof's apex, straddling it for security, a full moon pushes itself from a cloud. Honking v-shaped group of geese is frozen silhouetted against a racing moon as night soon overwhelms all. Now I can count geese as they fly across the moon's face, migrating south on a still fall night. I realize some, now passing before me overhead, will be filled with buck shot when attempting to alight in the frosty mourning air from their long journey.

[Scene]

Blue-helmeted cadre. Use Brazzo to clean latrine brass, private. Grass drill. Now jump like a rabbit. Maneuvers. Frost inside my boots, frozen mind, charge! Hurry it up. Attach bayonets. Parry to the left. Parry to the right. Thrust home. Charge. Kill! Evening approaches. I go over to my favorite cherry tree and scale its circumscribed bark, dark reddish and curl up here and there beckoning me to pull a trailing upturned piece around the branch. I strip it off. Grey becomes greyer. A chorus begins conducted by cicada. Er reee, er ree accompanied by chatter of tens of sparrows roosting in ivy-covered walls of our brick house. All sound stops. A flutter of clear plastic like membranous wings from an arm's reach away. A cicada has been sitting on the branch above me. It's gone to another tree.

But an incoming cicada plops itself beside me. On the downbeat, all begin to er reee er reee once again. I grab the locust above me. Er reee er ree intensifies. Its vibrations frighten me. I release it. And it goes into the evening dusk. The chatter of roosting sparrows stops.

[Scene]

Early morning, war is on, big guns sound over distant hills. Bog, fog, frozen leafs, crunching of boots pressing into half-frozen mud.

[Scene]

I remember it well. Christmas and I knew what my present would be. I asked for it and I would receive it. Depression days of 1939 or not—a Red Ryder bee-bee gun. The ultimate toy for a nine-year-old boy, the ultimate weapon in a boy's arsenal. Visiting my boyfriend's house, I don't remember his present. I just remember mine. I learned to spar around with my newly acquired gun.

It paid to wear thick corduroy trousers, the bee-bees stung at close range. I went deep into the neighboring woodlands. The stillness hung loud. The flicker of light patterns from leaves above. The patterns of brush leaves near the ground below. The humid heat. I stalked, I listened to the intense silence. And then abruptly above me moved a silent chickadee.

But what was a winter chickadee doing here in the heat of mid-summer? I aimed. I fired. It fell lifeless to the woodland's soft floor. I picked up the still warm body into my hand. Its eyes were now closed with its thick eyelids, lifeless, no cheerful chirping possible, no flittering about thickets, no anything. I had killed. The heat of the stillness swallowed me, nauseated me. Why had I killed? Why had I killed this pretty little bird? Would I ever kill again?

[Scene]

War. The rattle of machine guns to my left. Fog. Fog. More fog. The rattle of machine guns to my right.

[Scene]

Before me is the explosive flutter of a grouse under an apple tree from an old homestead orchard followed by an explosive blast from my shotgun. A bunch of us guys join up with the native lobstermen on a blistery day for some off shore sea duck hunting blasting away indiscriminately at ducks as we lie on rubbery slippery seaweed laden rock of some off shore islands. Cold, miserable smell of shot gun powder in the air as flock after flock would attempt to cozy up to our decoys. The dead would drift toward us to be cooked with turnips to relieve them of their fishy odor. The remaining would drift on out to sea for a non-ceremonial burial. Yes, I would and did kill again.

[Scene]

The whole hillside is blanketed in orange from the setting sunlight. Seven migratory ducks rise from the creek as I jog by, rising in formation with great acceleration. But one suddenly stops—the head dangling for a moment on the telephone line like a limp clown, then falling out of the air, its home is its safety. The sun is setting upon my timberland.

Tomorrow I will sell the timber rights to my stand of magnificent trees. I finish my bottle of wine and crawl into the backseat of the car. Red-winged blackbirds begin to roost in reeds near the car. At first there are only a few. Then there are hundreds upon hundreds and their noise becomes deafening. No questions. No ifs. No doubts. No possibilities.

It is revealed. At that moment I know. Among the deafening sound of the birds and the intense sunset covering all—God exists!

[Scene]

Grey fecal-brown mud meeting grey deathly grey sky at the horizon. Fix bayonets. Charge!

[Scene]

Thick mist condenses, freezing upon the brambles. A chickadee appears. Confused and startled As if it have returned from another place less earthly than here. Could it be a stranger in its own domain? Where have you been little chickadee?

FI

63. EXT/HOUSE—DAY

Konrad falls onto the hot cement of the veranda. He looks directly into the sun and continues to write in his mind some semi-lucid intervals to Ann. A showy Holomelina moth with its dull red and black wings and several marine blue butterflies flutter about the window sill, near the typewriter for a moment, and then disappear over the wall of the veranda. The next letter begins...

> KONRAD (Narrates while typing)

> Dear Ann...

64. INT/ROOM—DAY

[Scene]

> The crow of a Barbadian rooster awakens me, it reminds me, it haunts me, not of my early childhood memories but with noon walks to the sea with wind blowing your hair. I see you gay and full of life, vivacious and happy. The sun rises and light enters my tiny room. On the floor stands an empty pop bottle beside a newspaper. I must leave Barbados.

> The taxi whirls on winding roads through fields of tall cane, once again you are beside me, the wind blowing your hair, I reach to press it back over your ear, and you're gone!

65. INT/PLANE—DAY

> KONRAD (to himself)

> The flight to Antigua is short. I check the map. I could get out; wander to that plane sitting over there and fly back to you. It would be so simple. I look about me. I stand up to stretch, to stretch or to dream, to dream of walking off the plane as in

somnolence, to follow my emotions, not the mechanics of living, not the prescribed, dictated pathways, not schedules of schedules, but simply to wander away, to take flight to leave and find you. You're out there somewhere—I will find you. But no, I'm a prisoner of programming, programmed to humanity—to humanitarian, duty, goals, a slave of Christian thought. But, why not? Why not seek you, sweeping you into my arms and never letting go—you would understand my irrational behavior, because you will know why I am irrational . . . Love, Howard.

Dear Ann,

[Scene]

KONRAD (to himself)

The plane lifts into the air once more, I look into the empty skies attempting to understand the forces acting upon me—those terribly rational forces—those constraining forces that disallow heaven being on earth, love being easily grasped, tenderness being readily given to the one you love.

What evil powers are those that have left me sitting in the middle of the sky with stark emptiness? There, there she is, she's giggling—this is hardly the time for giggling my dear. I'm in a serious mood here—but you continue to laugh, it's alright, I understand and you're terribly cute so you can get away with anything. At least you're beside me once more. I'll be cleverer this time and try not to touch you.

I'll not lose you this time. What wild things shall we do my dear? Would you like to snorkel in the bay at Casablanca and then listen to raindrops on a tent in South Africa—dance in an Austrian beer garden before picking apple blossoms in a little German village—or just look into each others eyes and dream dreams?

Love, Konrad.

Dear Ann,

66. INT/PLANE—DAY

KONRAD

No, no coffee. Thank you. New York, reality, fasten your seat belts, gravity, force equals mass times acceleration.

KONRAD (to himself)

Sometime I must attempt to make poetry out of the Schrodinger wave equation. Now really, how can this be? How can the beauty of a psi-function of the wave equation remind me of you? I must be drunk. I am drunk—drunk with thoughts, all kinds of thoughts and now, I am beginning to coherently place them into perspective—from the moonlight upon your face, reflecting from the choppy waters, to the affection you show for others.

You're sweet. You're downright cute, or have I ever told you these things before? You are you. That is what others may have missed in knowing you. That you are beyond real description because you are definitely you. Most are only half you, a little bit of themselves, but you are magnanimous. And do you know something you don't even know just how wonderful you are. Think about it my dear.

Of course, by now you know why I am writing, writing, writing—to keep what little sanity I can cling to until the moment I will see you again. I must be clever, cleverer than ever before to pass the time into moments so that our lives together will seem as a flower not as separate petals. Just the word now conjures the fragrance of a flower from the island, and that leads to a lonely delightful afternoon at the café out over the bay, moments without that were a lifetime. Perhaps we did live a lifetime together--perhaps in other time frames. It was as much love and affection—but no—no it's not going to work—for I need you now.

Love, Konrad.

Dear Ann,

The tears are beginning once again—for just now I realize how little time I had spent gazing into your lovely eyes. Do you have any idea my dear how long I could look into your eyes? Sleep might eventually come to me, but I would simply be dreaming of looking into your eyes. All things come to an end but one—and that will continue forever. So I shall finish by saying hello dearest one, woman with the loveliest smile, the most charming lady of past, present and future.

Love, Howard.

Dear Ann,

New York is below—dazzling show of lights. I'm getting closer to you by the moment. Soon somehow I must travel to you. Maybe I will call you every night to hear your voice. Maybe you can join me somewhere, someplace near. I plan to see you everywhere, always pestering you to remind you that I exist, that I, in fact, more than exist. I'm learning to live, to love to romp in the joy of being, of being a loving, warm friendly guy and all because of you. Be patient.

I'm going to fly, fly to the moon and beyond, fly with me high, beyond the heavens, beyond the usual, to romantic places nestled amongst the stars, enjoy the music that transcends human thought, searching the unknown. We could try for it. Let's go for it. Life is here. We are here. Let there be no limits.

Suddenly Konrad's mind switches . . .

[Scene]

How she got her name The Scepter I really never knew, she was neither dignified nor sleek upon the sea, she was a retrofitted logger ship and bad to reach or come about, whose brown and heavy canvases slowed her something dreadfully, to go before the wind or tack, moored near the wharf she lapped the waves, and then would roll and creek to side, before to tip quite femininely, her barnacled and beaten bow, that April night was black indeed, we parted unaware, and set the diesel engine chugging, and backed her into the sea, with running lights a flicker, she timidly set forth, to meet the watery monsters with swells that rolled and broke, we flung her sails into position that seemed uneager and unable, that flapped and flapped so back and forth . . . bubbling champagne in Rio, those wild yacht parties in the Mediterranean, gamble at Monte Carlo, holding you close to me. We will overlook the plaza in Lima. I don't know, just everything, anything, let's experience it all, I want to live all lives, be all things, but only for your eyes, with you the lights of all the cities of the world will be ours. The faster the better, the higher, the faster, the more exciting the higher. From the common place, the mundane to the exotic, the fantastic the ultimate of experiences. Whatever your pleasures, whatever your needs, I shall satisfy them. I'll paint your nude portrait in an attic room in Paris. We'll have breakfast overlooking the Rhine. We'll steal a few token things from a Danish shop. We'll challenge the system, kick up our heels, sky dive, and fly an ultra-light. We'll attend the Russian ballet, mountain climb in the Andes, ski with the jet set dance at the carnival in Brazil, hold hands during boring speeches . . . the clouds drifted silently through a moonless sky, as stars guided us reluctantly along our darkened way, the wind rose fast and whitecaps eerily danced, upon the inky waters, as rope lines whipped and stretched and she began to heel, a stiff wind caught her mainsail and swirling waters, and her worn timbers shuddered, she balked as if to argue with the choppy swirling waters, and far ahead the lighthouse cried out an urgent message . . . help catch a rhinoceros for a zoo, blow up balloons for a children's benefit party, throw ice cream at each other, see which one can scream the loudest and then kiss till dawn.

You'll flash those dark brown eyes at me and I'll be able to do anything to prove my prowess. I'll have you smile at me and then, I'll go conduct an orchestra while moving a mountain and they said you could not grow bananas in the Antarctic. I'll show them the meaning of a smile. You're everything I need, my dream, the love of my life, I've met a king and a queen but they are mere nothings compared with you .

Love, Konrad.

Dear Ann,

If dreams come true, I will always be loving you. If dreams don't come true, I'll always be loving you. Dearest take care, watch out at intersections, don't talk to anyone, don't look at anyone, don't move, just breathe until I have you in my arms once more, take your vitamins, stay out of drafts. If I had any idea of how precious those moments were with you . . .

a crashing wave broke o'er her bow, and salty spray poured all around, our hands were white in thick wet gloves as water ran beneath our clothes, a breaking wave lashed Scepter's stern, the icy wind did stiffen, Scepter strained and moaned and pitched, as churning water struck with vengeance, to plunder the intruder. I adore you, I worship you, you are so very good, I miss you so much, but I miss more the things I've never known with you, waking up and seeing the sun's rays over your face.

I've never seen you asleep. I'm sure you're beautiful when you're asleep. I'll cuddle up to you and pet your hair. You would turn and open your eyes. It's overwhelming to me these possibilities, I must know them. I must experience them to sunbath together, to chase you to hold each other by the fireplace with flickering embers, ropes around our weakened waists lashed weary soul with soul, as both were now upon the wheel to keep her to the wind.

Dear Ann,

Just for you, the winter ice begins to thaw, cold winds blow through tall dead grass, the sun shines warmly upon my face, spring comes on forever, but this one will be the most beautiful of my life, the snowcapped mountains beckon me to listen to my heart, the buoy tipped to and then tipped fro, running past, it clanged the bell, and screamed its frantic warning—Gull Rock was dead ahead, the alpine crocus heralds the May showers, that will cause the meadows still patched with snow to soon be covered with brilliant color, I raise the lantern to shine its light, into the face of my fearful mate he shouted and yelled above the wind's roar, but drowned were his words for today and tomorrow, the pale blue sky with its caressing breezes, water and wood made a mix of debris, but how can I kiss you, the sounds of the wasps and bees busy with activity, the Scepter was struck with granite and wind I pray each night that somehow, someday, I will be allowed to love you, her bilge belched vast quantities of liquidity sea, I think about you all the time now, kissing you in my dreams, the old luger slid deeply down stern high, I wake up and realize I have been holding you, and silence remained with all three, for all things remind me of you...

FO

FI

67. EXT/HOUSE—DAY

Konrad stares into the turbulent waves crashing upon the rocks below the window, mumbling and unresponsive. Carlotta has called the hospital. Konrad leans heavily upon Carlotta and faintly whispers,

KONRAD

Dearest Carlotta, tell Ann that God has given me the chance to be with her at last. Let me say good-bye to my friends the waves from my Ensenada window—good-bye, dear friends. Strange how they keep their beauty yet never have loved

He danzando en madio de las estrallos para

solo un momento y nunca saber porque.

I have danced amongst the stars but only for a moment and never knew why.

THE END

V

CHINESE BLOSSOM NOTES

Registration # 1449768

Introduction

The author lived in Lanzhou, Gansu, China for two years and this play is designed to be a movie based on some of the impressions of that stay.

The film script would have voice overs by Chinese ethnics (San Francisco) of several ages. The filming is to be made in China. This would be a very inexpensive film to make.

Prefatory Note:

The attached short film-script is intended to be produced in the following manner and does not strictly conform to the standard screenplay format.

A series of scenes would be filmed in China by a Chinese studio in partnership with an American film producer. The voice overs (V.O.) usually accompany the specific scene. They are in poetic prose style. It would be done in English by a Chinese-accented girl's voice (with the exception of the first scene which is an older American man's voice).

The girl's voice and person should age within the film (from 10 to 29 years of age, probably requiring three different actors). The voice overs should also be separately done in Chinese to the same film scenes—thus made marketable in China.

The length of the film will be determined essentially by the length of the scenes. I estimate the length to be about an hour and twenty minutes.

[Scene]

West end of great wall fragments.

[Scene]

One room school house with one bedroom for teacher on top of a hill. Fine snow is falling. Garden wall surrounds school house. Wall is seen from inside bedroom window.

V.O. (70 yr. old western man)

OLD MAN

Dear Ling-Li,

The sky is getting grayer now. A soft fine snow lies upon the garden wall outside my window and the time has come for me to say good-bye.

I remember so well, that first day on my arrival to the village. I had come to teach but really to search for the mysterious truth of reality that I believed lay hidden in some little earthen village such as yours—through your eyes I would discuss these truths. You were the last blossoms of my life.

Old One

[Scene]

Tree blossom petals lying on ground

OLD MAN

The petals now lie disintegrating.
Xie xie and zai jian, Old One

[Scene]

Girl herding seven sheep

V.O. Girl's [(16 yr. old) voice with heavy Chinese accent.]

LING-LI

Dear Old One,

Bright sky, cool morning air, May in China. I am almost sixteen years old now, but it was surely only a moment ago .I run the path as fast as I can- wonderful, wonderful day. Soon my chores will begin- the seven sheep to be herded to the dumpsite for munching. But surely this glorious spring day can bring nothing but pure joy to my heart. I know the world is full of wonderment and I will taste today, the enchantment of life, as never before. Ling Li

[Scene]

Close up of pink and green apple buds. Flock of swallows.

V.O.

LING-LI

Dear Old One,

The pink-green apple buds are preparing to burst. A small flock of swallows flutter and settle, flutter and settle as I dance the path toward the houses below. Ling Li

[Scene]

Girl dancing on path above a few rural houses

LING-LI

Dear Old One,

My eyes try to see everything, my mind tries to think everything and even my lips try to whistle. I remember the heavens had a surprise for me that day. Ling Li

[Scene]

Close up of eyes and lips of girl as she tries to whistle.

[Scene]

Pigeons with wooden whistles attached to wings with whistling sounds as they dive by.

[Scene]

Middle-aged man in western attire/suit and one hand-luggage walking up path towards school house

V.O.

LING-LI

Dear Old One,

Politely you came, "ni hao." My "ni hao" followed, I am ashamed to say, with slight embarrassment, and my eyes must have turned away from you. Ling Li

[Scene]

Close ups of man's cane striking rhythmically on ground and girl's hemp slippers flopping on dirt path.

V.O.

LING-LI

Dear Old One,

Your stick clicked upon the rocky path with a certain rhythm as my sandals clopped with another. We passed. I wonder if your thoughts turned to me after our greeting. I know my thoughts quickened to a fascination with the stranger from beyond the horizon where I had never been. Yes, Old One, I remember that day well—I will always treasure it. Ling Li.

[Scene]

Poplar trees in light breeze beginning to leaf out.

V.O.

LING-LI

Dear Old One,

The poplar trees begin to form young leaflets that glisten when moved by the breeze. My bones are young like the poplar leaves. I used to feel very sorry for you Old One, but now I realize that to have become old, is a proud thing and to be able to reflect upon your life and its moments is a thing of beauty. Ling-Li

[Scene]

Girl with teacher walking among poplars with sun glistening through.

V.O.

LING-LI

Dear Old One,

I hope that one of those moments was the time we spent walking through the poplars with the October sun warming our faces. You see me, but you also see through my eyes. Is it not so? You told me your eyes could see but few things. Ling-Li

[Scene]

Close ups of girl's eyes and old man's eyes.

V.O.

LING-LI

Dear Old One,

I think you saw more with your old eyes than many with young eyes. I walk in those poplars with you now, even though you are not really here with me. And I talk with you to be able to understand. I think many times I understand.

Ling-Li

[Scene]

Snow on mountain top.

V.O.

LING-LI

Dear Old One,

Snow still remains on the tops of the mountains. Ling-LI

[Scenes]

Children going into schoolhouse. Children sitting inside school room. Rainy day outside of schoolhouse.

V.O.

LING-LI

Dear Old One,

It is a cold day. I think of today like the day I saw you again. We, the children of the village, had gone to our schoolhouse many times that month always hoping to find a teacher waiting there for us. The day was cold and rainy. The hard dirt path had turned up slippery. My heart was sad, for how on such a day could there be any brightness?

Ling Li

[Scene]

Teacher inside schoolroom talking.

V.O.

LING-LI

Dear Old One,

But it happened! It was you! My face must have been like a candle, I felt it glowing. I learned little that day, but listened hard to your every sound.

[Scene]

Girl walking up muddy path with wet tree blossoms

V.O.

LING LI

On the way back up the muddy path I noticed how happy the cold wet blossoms were. Ling-Li

[Scene]

Light snow on poplar forest. Clear sky shot. Girl looking into morning clear sky.

V.O.

LING-LI

Dear Old One,

A light snow fell upon the yellow-green of Spring last night. The sky is clear this morning. I gaze upon the day sky, knowing what many others do not—the stars are burning brightly even though I do not see them. Well do I remember with fascination, when you told us at the schoolhouse about the stars. You said we live among the stars and from then on, I felt warm and not alone. Thank you for that. Ling-Li

[Scene]

Man eating bowl of soup with girl and parents in peasant's home kitchen.

V.O.

LING-LI

Dear Old One,

You know so much, Old One. Did you know that the soup you had at our house, soon after you arrived, had frog leg meat in it?

Ling-Li

V.O.

LING-LI

Dear Old One,

You taught me how to enjoy words. What a thrill it was when you showed me how to make English words in rhythm with each other. Ling-Li

[Scene]

Teacher reading from book in class.

V.O.

LING-LI

Dear Old One,

I could see the delight upon your face as you read the words from a small book to the class. I wrote such words put in this way. They were not as good as the ones you read us that day. I still have them. Do you remember them Old One? Ling Li

[Scene]

Peach blossoms, stars, dawn, more blossoms.

V.O.

LING-LI

Peach blossoms
Fade into dusk then reappear
As stars in the sky and dawn erases

The stars to create
The blossoms again

Ling-Li

[Scene]

Wet cold day. Girl brings hot water into teacher's bedroom. Teacher in bed.

V.O.

LING-LI

Dear Old One,

Today is wet and cold. Do you remember the day you were cold and miserable? I came to your room to give you some hot water. Even though you were sick you took the time to give me two words—magic and solitude. Ling-Li

[Scene]

Girl dreams of words floating in space.

V.O.

LING-LI

Magic, fantasy, an explosion of words. I dream of thousands of words floating about me, exciting words, beautiful words, strange words—all new, asking me to follow them into the spaces of . . . I awake.

V.O.

LING LI

Dear Old One,

Solitude—Oh yes, I understood the wonderful silence of just listening to the breezes near the stop of the hill—alone yet near someone or something. Sometimes, listening to the glass chimes in the wind brought loneliness—a solitude to me.

Thank you Old One for those two words. Ling-Li

[Scene]

Girl and girlfriend walking and skipping to village on warm sunny day.

V.O. (Chinese girl 14 yrs. Old)

LING-LI

Dear Old One,

Today I am happy. It was warm and sunny so I walked to the south village with my girl friend Ti. Ling.Li

[Scene]

Two girls walking and skipping down path, road, tall grass field, bridge, and sandbar.

V.O.

LING-LI

Bright the walk, happy the skip . . . down the path, on the road . . . through the tall grass, over the bridge, across the sand bar, stepping stone—over the creek, into the woods . . . up the hill, by the farmhouse . . . onto the road again.

[Scene]

Grain being thrashed by motor traffic on road of small country town and being attended by a few farmers on side of road.

[Scene]

Village market place with white—capped Muslims carrying things.

V.O.

LING-LI

Dear Old One,

The village was alive with white-capped Muslims carrying their loads. Soon we were upon the marketers with their various goods.
Ling Li

[Scene]

Close ups of red and green peppers, baskets, shoes, birds in cages, green and yellow apples, goldfish, cinnamon, cloves, and mushrooms.

V.O.

LING-LI

Red pepper, green pepper . . . baskets galore . . . new shoes, old shoes . . . birds in their cages . . . green apples, yellow apples . . . goldfish too . . . cinnamon here, cloves there, mushrooms piled about . . . all around us,

[Scene]

The two girls eating Sichuan meat on skewers, squawking chickens, pig carcasses hanging from hook, close up of girl friend eating candied apple, close up of girl holding plastic bag with a gold fish.

V.O.

                            LING-LI

> All about us . . . good things to eat, candied this, fire-cooked that . . . smell the burning fat . . . talk and noise . . . squawking chickens, meat hanging from a hook . . . What to buy with our yuan?

[Scene] Close up of Chinese money.

What to do with our day? We are having great fun. Ti ate candied fruit and I now have "Chong-Yu" . . . a goldfish.

[Scene] Young man on street corner fixing bicycle tires.

[Scenes]

Girl writing poem on table, rain on girl's bedroom window, melon field near a river, girl by stove reading book .

V.O.

                            LING-LI

> Dear Old One,
>
> The rain hits against the window, so I did not work in our seed-melon field. You remember, the one near the river. Ling-Li

[Scene]

V.O.

LING-LI

Dear Old One,

After my chores in the house I sat by the stove where the dull afternoon light struck the pages and I read over and over your poem—

[Scene]

Apple blossoms swaying in wind, stars, sun, moon, apple blossom petals

V.O.

[Scene]

Apple blossoms floating down and mixing with peach blossoms

V.O.

LING-LI

CHINESE APPLE BLOSSOMS

Delicate
Swaying in the winds of time
Reflecting the light
From near stars, sun and moon
Apple blossom petals,
Showering about
Bring eternal renewal
Of beauty and freshness

To air and mind
Chinese blossoms seen by Chinese eyes
Mystic blossoms, petals of philosophy
Blossoming over eons and dynasties
Chinese blossoms ever, ever lasting

LING-LI

Dear Old One,

It is as if it were snowing for I do not hear the rain as your apple blossoms and my peach blossoms form a wonderful picture in my mind.

Ling-Li

[Scene]

Fireworks, people shuffling about in area of fireworks.

V.O. {l6 year old girl)

LING-LI

Dear Old One,

It was a night of the Spring Festival—Fireworks aglow, rockets lighting the blue black sky.

[Scenes]

Girl meeting boy, activity of preparation for wedding, sewing, embroidery hooking, making cloth shoes, banquet scene, close up of girl's sad face.

V.O.

LING LI

Dear Old One,

Relatives from far and near. Was a night my cousin Cui met a boy from the village nearby. But alas it made little difference for Jinqun was to be her groom. Cui finished after Junior High—no money to go on with-sad although intelligent, she was of age to be at housework. And now at twenty would be married to Jinqun. She prepared unhappily but most diligently for her wedding day. Knitting and sewing, embroidery and hooking. Then to make her cloth shoes. Finally her new dress did her mother make. The banquet, big and many attended. Jinqun's place was quite a stir But Cui's face hid her sorrow on this her wedding day.

Ling-Li

[Scene]

Girl writing letter to man.

V.O. (17 year old girl)

Dear Old One,

Great news! I'm off to Lanzhou to an essay competition.

[Scene]

University of Lanzhou University campus and inside scene of professor in winter coat and scarf on lecturing. Broken glass window with hole beside his lectern. Ling Li

[Scene]

Girl is handed an award at essay ceremony

V.O. (20 year old girl)

LING-LI

Dear Old One,

My preliminary essay won the district, so now I'm away. I'm soaring I have been searching and now I am to respond I have ideas. I have words. Now I can explore the heavens to create where nothing stood before. To form a phrase never used before. This then is the meaning of life. Wish me well 'Old One' for I seek high places

Ling-Li

[Scene] Inside shot of Chinese bookstore and close up of opened Chinese novel pages.

V.O.

LING-LI

Dear Old One,

You once told me you thought the world was mine I wondered what that meant. It may be happening I received the top award for my essay I feel the world is now mine I feel warm all over I feel a great kindness to a humanity and to my people—the Chinese.

Ling-Li

[Scene] Great Buddha Statue

Can all of this be happening? It seems only moments ago that I began to write. Now the world is opening its doors to me. You pointed me in a direction that led me to the universe of words. How can I ever repay you Old One?

Ling-Li

[Scene]

Busy bicycle traffic in street.

[Scene]

Girl opening up mail from Beijing University

V.O. (22 year old girl)

LING LI

Dear Old One,

There's more. Where will it lead me and when will it end? I have been notified that I am to receive a two year scholarship to Beijing University to study Chinese literature and composition.

Ling-Li

[Scene]

Birds flying, wind blowing trees, sky and clouds, flowers, and rain.

[Scene]

Bamboo forest in Bamboo Park.

V.O. (24 yr. old girl)

LING-LI

Dear Old One,

Now the birds must fly higher. Now the wind must blow harder. Now the sky must become taller to reach where I feel I am. The flowers are more beautiful this spring. The showers are more gentle. The meaning to all things has taken on a new depth. The emotion within me will surely fuel a life time of writing. Ling-Li

[Scene]

Girl writing at desk at night by lamp.

V.O. (26 yr. old girl)

LING-LI

Dear Old One,

It has been a long time since I have written to you. I want next to write to tell you of my first novel. I finished it last night. So now I must write you—you, the one that has written me so faithfully through the years should be the first to know. Your letters have kept my thoughts creative.

Ling-Li

[Scene]

Girl mailing copy of her novel manuscript.

V.O.

LING-LI

Dear Old One,

Now my first novel is done I call it 'A Summer in Wei Village'. And I am sending you a copy. I know you cannot read anymore, but have your friend, whom you have spoken of, read it to you. As you listen, remember every word is part of you. Ling-Li

[Scene]

Generic shot of Beijing.

[Scene]

Girl with good looking young man walking in Beijing together.

[Scene]

Same girl and boy eating at restaurant with close up of glass cage behind where they are seated that is full of snakes to be eaten.

V.O.

LING-LI

Dear Old One,

Of course you would be the first to tell me it would happen. I have met a wonderful young man. His name is Yen Qiang. We saw each other across a conference room in Beijing he is studying Chinese literature at Jo Tong University in Xi-an. But unlike me is interested in historical aspects. We spent a great deal of time together this summer. And he will visit me during the Spring Festival. I know this relationship may lead to conflict-conflict to my life of writing but I being human must breath and love.

Ling Li

V.O.

LING LI

Dear Old One,

My second novel 'Tomorrow Comes Today' has won international acclaim. I am to go New York to Receive the "Writer's Guild Award." I have been recognized. My life has been rewarded, fulfilled and made meaningful. And I have managed to give something in return. Can I ask for more? I think not. I know my thoughts are limited. But my emotions seem to wrap around these simple thoughts that push them into significance. I will continue to write you 'Old One', even though I know you can neither read my letters nor write me letters anymore for you are, far, far, far...

Ling-Li

[Scene]

Generic shot of New York City.

[Scene]

Leaves falling in NYC Central park with girl walking in park path.

V.O. (29 yr. old girl)

LING-LI

Dear Old One,

Many leaves have fallen since I've heard from you I know why you do not write me anymore, but it doesn't seem to help. Yes 'Old One' I remember that day well and I will treasure it. Ling Li

THE END

Printed in the United States
By Bookmasters